Nov 1938

Mrs. ...

D1132859

THE SECRET OF CHRISTIAN JOY

The Secret of Christian Joy

By

VANCE HAVNER

Author of "By the Still Waters"

New York

Fleming H. Revell Company

London and Edinburgh

New York: 158 Fifth Avenue
London: 21 Paternoster Square

PREFACE

IN this day of the making of many books one hesitates to add another volume to the number. We have been encouraged, however, by the readers of these sermon-articles as they appeared in various magazines to collect them in permanent form. So we send them forth again with the earnest desire that they may glorify Him Who loved us and gave Himself for us.

Grateful acknowledgment is made for the kind permission granted by several magazines for the reprinting of the following:

To *Revelation,* Philadelphia, Pennsylvania, and *Serving-and-Waiting* (now included in *Revelation*) for " Old Time Religion," " The Secret of Christian Joy," " Revive Us Again," " The Foolishness of God," and " Is It Nothing to You? "

To *Moody Monthly,* Chicago, Illinois, for " The Heavenly Vision."

To *King's Business,* Los Angeles, California, for " Let God Be True," " Learning, Living, Looking," and " He Is Beside Himself."

V. H.

Charleston, S. C.

CONTENTS

I

THE SECRET OF CHRISTIAN JOY

HE Church suffers today from a saddening lack of old-fashioned, simple-hearted, overflowing, Christian joy. We have plenty of knowledge, plenty of enthusiasm and denominational zeal, but Christians and churches that started out in revival fires are living in the smoke, and the " amens " and " hallelujahs " have gone from most assemblies of the saints.

When one recalls that we are to rejoice in the Lord always —and then looks in on the average Sunday congregation, he realizes that something has happened to us since Pentecost. We meet on the Lord's day more as though we had assembled to mourn a defeat than to celebrate a victory.

Although the New Testament centers in a cross and is bathed in the blood of martyrs and blackened by the fires of persecution, its note from beginning to end is one of triumphant joy. It begins with an angel chorus and ends with rejoicing around the throne of God. The Gospel means " good news." Our Lord's characteristic greeting was, "*Be of good cheer.*" He gave us " three cheers ": the cheer of forgiveness, "*Be of good cheer, thy sins be forgiven thee*" (Matthew 9: 2); the cheer of companionship, "*Be of good cheer: it is I; be not afraid*" (Mark 6: 50); the cheer of victory, "*Be of good cheer; I have overcome the world*" (John 16: 33). He invited us to a feast, not to a funeral. He said, "*If ye know these things, happy are ye if ye do them,"* and He intended that His joy should remain in us and that our joy should be full.

When we enter the life of the early Church, we find them eating their meat with gladness and singleness of heart, praising God. We follow Paul from prison to prison, but his shout is, "*Rejoice in the Lord alway; and again I say, Rejoice.*" Evidently emotion had not been outlawed among the saints in those days. Today the same church member who yells like a Comanche Indian at a football game sits like a wooden Indian in the house of God on Sunday. When David danced before the returning ark his wife despised him and was smitten with barrenness. Today happy Christians are frowned upon by those dismal souls who thus proclaim their spiritual barrenness. In the temple Pharisees complained because the children cried their " hosannas " around the Saviour (Matthew 21: 12–16). Hilarious, child-hearted Christians have always brought down the scorn of those who measure piety by the length of the face.

Sometimes one thinks the text most suitable for a sermon to the average church congregation would be Galatians 4: 15: "*Where is then the blessedness ye spake of?* " If we were absolutely truthful, would we not have to sing as our experience?—

> *" Where is the blessedness I knew*
> *When first I saw the Lord?*
> *Where is the soul-refreshing view*
> *Of Jesus and His Word?*
> *What peaceful hours I then enjoyed!*
> *How sweet their memory still!*
> *But they have left an aching void*
> *This world can never fill."*

In John 20: 20 we read: "*Then were the disciples glad,*

when they saw the Lord." Here we have the secret of Christian joy: it turns upon those two words, "then" and "when." We are glad when we see the Lord.

It does not read, "Then were the disciples glad when they saw themselves." When we see the Lord we see ourselves, but what we see is not very complimentary. Job saw the Lord and abhorred himself. Daniel saw the Lord and his comeliness was turned to corruption. Isaiah saw the Lord and cried, "*Woe is me!*" Habakkuk saw the Lord and his body trembled and rottenness entered his bones. Saul of Tarsus fell in the dust and John fell at the feet of the Lord as one dead. Some of us do not see the Lord because we are looking at ourselves, and so doing we are never glad.

You will observe, next, that our verse does not say, "Then were the disciples glad when they saw each other." Looking at other Christians is a most disappointing business. Peter always is tempted to wonder about John and needs the Lord's stern word, "What is that to thee? Follow me yourself." We read in I John 5: 16: "*If any man see his brother sin a sin which is not unto death, he shall ask, and he shall give him life for them that sin not unto death.*" Our brother's sin is not a challenge to criticism but a call to prayer. When Christians begin to watch each other they do not see the Lord.

Nor were these disciples glad when they saw their circumstances. Their circumstances were not very encouraging, with the doors shut for fear of the Jews. All through the Word we find God's men grieved over circumstances, but when they see the Lord they rejoice (Psalm 41: 4–13; Lamentations 5: 19–22; Micah 7: 1–7). Consider Habakkuk. He was perplexed over the prosperity of the wicked and the sufferings of the righteous. God did not explain this, but when Habakkuk saw the Lord he could say, "*Whatever the circumstances, I will joy in the God of my salvation.*" Then was Habakkuk glad when he saw the Lord.

We do not even read that the disciples were glad when they saw a particular doctrine about the Lord. It is possible to know many things about the Lord without seeing Him. Believers go off at tangents and perch on favourite spokes of the wheel of truth, instead of standing at the hub. Some see only the work of the Spirit, forgetting that the Spirit testifies of Christ. Some look to the Lord's return with an academic interest in an event rather than a joyful expectation of a Person. Others harp on the abundant or victorious life (which is simply Christ in the believer) in a fashion which often sees a life more than it sees the Lord.

In a day when false Christs are being preached it is well to notice that this Christ Who brought such joy to His disciples was a crucified Christ, bearing the marks of the Cross, "*wounded for our transgressions and bruised for our iniquities.*" Enemies of the Cross of Christ would ridicule the Blood and cover His hands and side, but we are truly glad only when we see the crucified Lord.

But He was also a risen Lord. Christ crucified is not enough. If He rose not, our preaching is vain, we are yet in our sins and of all men most miserable. And how many Christians there are who claim to be dead with Christ, but who are not living in the power of His Resurrection!

Now consider what a change our Lord wrought when He appeared. He found the disciples huddled in a room with the doors shut for fear (John 20: 19). Hundreds of believers live today behind closed doors of dread and uncertainty. They are afraid of life and of death, of the devil, of criticism, of circumstances, afraid of today and tomorrow, imprisoned in fear, doubt and worry. They need to see the Lord.

First, our Lord brought assurance: He established before the disciples the fact of His resurrection. The report of it had seemed too good to be true. Several times in the Word we read of the people believing not for joy: Jacob about Joseph (Genesis 45: 26), the disciples at our Lord's appearance (Luke 24: 41), and Rhoda at the deliverance of Peter (Acts 12: 14). Somewhere I have read of a little tenement child, accustomed to sharing one glass of milk with several others, being given a large glass of milk in a hospital. Clutching it eagerly, the little fellow asked, "Please, nurse, how deep may I drink?" Often the good things of God seem almost too good to be true. And how wonderful is the Divine mathematics that all things are for me and yet all things are for you! I am sure I could not divide a thousand dollars among a multitude so that each would receive a thousand dollars. But the grace of God is in no wise diminished by sharing, it is all for each!

So our Lord brings assurance, as if to say, "Yes, I am really alive, there is no mistake. And because I live, ye shall live also." If on any point you lack assurance, it is because you are not seeing the Lord. *"Be not faithless, but believing."*

Then He brought joy. He had promised, *"I will see you again, and your heart shall rejoice, and your joy no man taketh from you"* (John 16: 22). This joy of the Lord is a full joy, not partial; it is a remaining joy, not a fleeting emotion that comes and goes; and no one may take it from us. That is our Lord's answer to those poor souls who are always asking, "Yes, but will it last?" We are glad when we see the Lord, and the measure of our joy is in proportion to our faith by which we look unto Jesus. There is nothing fanciful and hit-or-miss about it. As we look unto Him we are lightened and our faces are not ashamed.

Our Lord also brought to these disciples a commission: "*As my Father hath sent me, even so send I you.*" The joy of the Lord is not merely for personal enjoyment, He gives to us freely that we may freely give. God gives us the joy of salvation, expecting that then we will teach transgressors His ways. After Peter was converted, he was to strengthen the brethren and feed the sheep. After we see the fair King, we should see the far country of service in His Name. Judson saw the Lord—and he saw Burma. Hudson Taylor saw the Lord—and he saw China. Moody saw the Lord—and he saw a lost world. After Saul asked, "*Who art thou, Lord?*" he asked, "*What wilt thou have me to do?*" After the vision comes the venture. As our Lord was sent forth, so sends He us.

Next, our Lord brought to the disciples power: "*He breathed on them, and saith unto them, Receive ye the Holy Ghost.*" Whatever interpretation you put upon that, there is a bequeathing of power. There would be no use in giving joy if there were no power to sustain it, no use in giving a commission if there were no power to carry it through. After David prayed, "*Restore unto me the joy of thy salvation,*" he was careful to add, "*Uphold me with thy free spirit.*"

And He also gave them authority: "*Whose soever sins ye remit, they are remitted unto them; and whose soever sins ye retain, they are retained.*" However you explain this, it is evident that great authority is here delegated. If we saw the Lord, we would speak with authority and not as the scribes. We see sermon helps and commentaries but not the

Lord, and there is no note of heavenly unction. Here many a timid Timothy will find the cure for pulpit bashfulness: "*They looked unto him, and were lightened, AND THEIR FACES WERE NOT ASHAMED.*" Of course, there is a false courage, a brazen bravado which enters the pulpit with head thrown back, like Napoleon crossing the Alps. He who sees the Lord speaks with heavenly authority, not his own.

But perhaps someone complains: "Ah, yes, I know that seeing the Lord Jesus brings all these benefits, but, alas, He does not appear now as He did then so that we actually may see Him." That is why the Holy Spirit follows this account in John 20 with the record of doubting Thomas. He knew there would be Thomases through the ages who must see to believe. Has it ever occurred to you that you and I who see Him not as the disciples saw Him have a greater blessing declared from His own lips: "*Blessed are they that have not seen, and yet have believed*"? Though now we see Him not, yet believing, we rejoice with joy unspeakable and full of glory.

We are glad only when and as we see the Lord. It is according to our faith, as looking unto Jesus we see no man save Jesus only. There are many things that we see NOT YET—"*we see not yet all things put under him, but we see Jesus.*" And one day, when we see no longer through a glass as in a riddle, we shall see Him as He is. His servants shall serve Him and shall see His face.

A minister who was failing to preach Christ found a note in the pulpit Bible one Sunday morning. It read, "Sir, we would see Jesus." Convicted, he began to hold up the Lord in his messages. Some time later he found another note in the Bible reading, "*Then were the disciples glad when they saw the Lord.*"

It is the supreme need of the hour that believers should look away from all else, much of which may be good, and see only the Lord. Then shall we have fresh assurance and joy, we shall receive a new commission, with power and authority to carry it out. Robertson of Brighton, discouraged, once offered in prayer to resign his commission to preach. The Lord answered that what he needed was not to resign it, but to have it re-signed with Divine power and approval.

Remember that you cannot reach the "THEN" of our text without first coming to the "WHEN." *"THEN were the disciples glad WHEN they saw the Lord."*

II

"LET GOD BE TRUE"

"*Let God be true, but every man a liar.*"—ROMANS 3: 4.

IN my early Christian experience I set out to read the Bible with all the zeal of the average young believer, taking the promises at face value, believing the Scriptures as I found them, without benefit of footnotes and commentaries. I began with Genesis and was claiming the promises for myself when I encountered a Bible student from somewhere who informed me that those promises were not for me but for the Jews!

It had been evident to me in reading the Scriptures, as it must be to any prayerful student, that certain divine commitments relate particularly to Israel. But the restraint which my well-meaning friend placed upon my appropriation of spiritual truth for myself caused a sudden dampening of my ardour. Then I moved over into the New Testament and began appropriating the blessings of the Sermon on the Mount, and again I was interrupted and duly notified that all those things belonged to the Kingdom age! Next, I began in Acts and was moving along, daring to believe that I might claim some, if not all, of the powers that flowed from Pentecost, when I was again reminded that the Acts covered a transitional period and we were not to press those matters too literally!

I knew they would not let me have Revelation, since it

was concerning the future; so only the Epistles were left me. By the time I had made allowances for Greek roots and marginal references and contradictory footnotes, I came out in the same dilemma in which many Bible Christians find themselves today. I did not know which promises really were mine. I could not stand with confidence at any place in the Scriptures, lest some divider of the Word come along like a policeman to order me off private property and inform me that my verse did not mean just what it said, or that it was meant for someone else.

The outgrowth of it all has been a deep conviction that Bible Christians suffer today from the double error of making the Scriptures fit their own *explanations* on one hand, or their own *experiences* on the other. We spend much time denouncing modernism, and surely we ought to say with Paul, *“Though we, or an angel from heaven, preach any other gospel . . . let him be accursed.”* But sometimes I am not so afraid of modernist doubt from without as I am afraid of fundamentalist unbelief from within. By fundamentalist unbelief I mean that strange species of unbelief which loudly declares the Scriptures to be God-breathed, but immediately turns around and sets about adjusting the Bible to the limitations of our logic and our lives.

First, we endeavour to adjust the Scriptures to our own explanations. Mythology tells us of the bed of Procrustes. If a man was too short, he was stretched until he would fit the bed. If he was too long, his legs were chopped off until he would fit it. Do we not first decide what we are going to believe about the Bible, then size and sort the Scriptures, stretch them out or lop them off to fit the Procrustean beds of our private systems of interpretation? We come across a promise that glitters like a diamond on velvet. But we dare not accept it as it stands until we get down several books to find what this man and that one thinks it means.

After God called him, Paul conferred not with flesh and blood (Galatians 1: 16). But when God speaks to us, we do confer first with flesh and blood; we consult the authorities! And by the time we have paid tribute at all the tollgates of private interpretation and have looked at the Scriptures through the spectacles of a dozen disagreeing expositors, we come out with "loads of learned lumber in our heads," but unable to build from it all any worthy structure. Instead of asking, "What saith the Scripture?" we ask, "What say the scholars about the Scripture?" We are like one who would miss the sentiment of a love letter through studying its syntax.

Besides, if the Bible were so puzzling that one could not know it until the scholars explained it, what would become of the common people who could not go to schools nor buy heavy sets of commentaries?

> *"I have a life with Christ to live;*
> *But, ere I live it, must I wait*
> *Till learning can clear answer give*
> *To this and that book's date?*
>
> *"I have a life with Christ to live,*
> *A death with Christ to die;*
> *And must I wait till science give*
> *All doubts a clear reply?"*

No! And neither should we fall into the grievous error of missing what the Bible says by forever trying to pour it into this and that mould of private explanation.

On the other hand, we err in adjusting the Scriptures to fit the limitations of our own experiences. We look at a glowing promise or declaration, then we look around at what we call "facts," and if the facts do not seem to bear out the Scriptures, we make the Scriptures fit the facts instead of demanding that the facts rise to the level of the Scriptures.

We whittle down the Scriptures to fit experience. We read that "*whosoever is born of God sinneth not.*" Then we look around and say: "But yonder is a born-again believer who is living in sin," and thus we seek to adjust the Bible to experience. We read that the prayer of faith shall heal the sick. But we know somebody who was sick and prayed in faith, yet died. The facts do not seem to bear out the Scriptures, and we adjust the Book to the Procrustean bed of our pitiful experience. We dare not believe God's own bold words; we run them through a process to match our miserable faith—or lack of faith—and we are as guilty of denaturing the Scriptures as modernism ever dared to be.

We must believe what God said because God said it, not because logic or life seems to verify it. To be sure, the Bible is both reasonable and livable, but first of all it is so simply because God said so, and God's saying so makes it so. We must accept that or else go blundering along half-doubting, trying to mix the wisdom of man with "*the foolishness of God*" (I Corinthians 1: 25). God has spoken and that settles it: "*Let God be true, but every man a liar*" (Romans 3: 4). To doubt God and believe human explanation and experience is to make God a liar. If anybody has lied, man has lied. If there is any doubt on any point, give God the benefit of the doubt. If circumstances seem to contradict what God has said, let God be true and circumstances be liars. If scholars doubt what God has written, let God be true and let scholars be liars. If feelings do not seem to confirm the Word, let God be true and let feelings be liars. If we do not live up to what God has said, let God be true and let us be the liars.

"*He hath said . . . so that we may boldly say,*" and whatever contradicts Him is of the devil who is a liar and the father of it. When Satan entered human life, he took the form of a serpent and his question was, "*Yea, hath God said . . . ?*" When the Saviour came to earth, He took the form of a servant, and His answer in life and teaching was, "*Yea, God hath said.*"

God has said: "*There is no difference: For all have sinned, and come short of the glory of God.*" Men say that there is a difference and that sin is only arrested development, immaturity, biological growing pains. Whom shall we believe? "*Let God be true, but every man a liar.*"

God has said: "*Christ died for our sins according to the scriptures*"; "*was raised again for our justification*"; "*there is none other name under heaven given among men, whereby we must be saved.*" Men say that other ways are just as good. Modern Naamans claim that Abana and Pharpar are as good as Jordan. They do not like the Gospel of No Other Name. "*Let God be true, but every man a liar.*"

God says: "*He that believeth on the Son hath everlasting life: and he that believeth not the Son shall not see life; but the wrath of God abideth on him.*" Men believe in a sentimental God Who would wink at man's wickedness, and they forget that while God is love, He is also a consuming Fire. "*Let God be true, but every man a liar.*"

God says: "*Present your bodies a living sacrifice*"; "*come out from among them, and be ye separate.*" Men do not choose the highway of holiness; they would mix light with darkness and join Christ with Belial. But God has spoken, and he that believeth hath no part with an infidel. "*Let God be true, but every man a liar.*"

God says: "*Be filled with the Spirit.*" Men have dodged and denied the Bible doctrine of a definite enduement of power for service. They have been willing to miss a blessing rather than give up a prejudice. Painted fire has supplanted Pentecostal fire, and Samson, fresh from the lap of Delilah, shakes himself and knows not that the Spirit has departed from him. But it is not by might nor power, but by the Spirit of the Lord of hosts: "*Let God be true, but every man a liar.*"

God has said that Jesus shall return in the same manner as He went away. Scoffers ask, "Where is the promise of His coming?" Hypocrites read the face of the sky but cannot discern the signs of the times. Belshazzar drinks before his lords in ungodly revelry while astrologers and soothsayers guess at the meaning of the handwriting on the wall. We live in the Saturday evening of the age; the mystery of lawlessness heads up toward its awful climax; the night of apostasy darkens; the sky is lurid with the flames of approaching judgment. Jesus is coming! "*Let God be true, but every man a liar.*"

So, no matter which way we look, the issue is this: Are we to believe what God has said or the testimony of man? In Matthew 22:29, our Lord said: "*Ye do err, not knowing the scriptures, nor the power of God.*" We err because instead of knowing the Scriptures on the one hand we substitute explanations; and instead of God's power we substitute our experiences. And what can be more pathetic than to spend a lifetime expounding the supernatural without ever having experienced the supernatural, contending for the miracles of yesterday, yet practically denying the possibility of miracles today!

After all, the Word of God yields its deepest secrets not to scholarly analysis but to simple faith that dares to "*let God be true, but every man a liar.*" After the wise and prudent, even among the orthodox, have argued at length over this verse and that, God raises up some nonentity who dares to believe God's bold, brave words, and puts all the rest of us to shame. Few of us ever stand with all our weight on the Word of God. We pretend to, but in a crisis we usually make some concession to human weakness, and the Word does not profit us as it might, being mixed with unbelief in us who hear it.

In the thick of an engagement someone cried to the captain: "The flag is far ahead, and the regiment has fallen 'way behind the colours. Shall we bring the flag back to the regiment?"

The captain shouted back: "No! Bring the regiment up to the flag!"

We Bible Christians have fallen far behind our colours. Shall we bring the Scriptures back to us, trim them to suit our unbelief? Let us rather catch up with the Scriptures, both in our explanations and our experiences! "*Let God be true, but every man a liar.*"

III

"REVIVE US AGAIN"

"Wilt thou not revive us again: that thy people may rejoice in thee?"—PSALM 85: 6.

THE greatest need of America is an old-fashioned, heaven-born, God-sent revival. Throughout the history of the Church, when clouds have hung lowest, when sin has seemed blackest and faith has been weakest, there have always been a faithful few who have not sold out to the devil nor bowed the knee to Baal, who have feared the Lord and thought upon His Name and have not forsaken the assembling of themselves together. These have besought the Lord to revive His work in the midst of the years, and in the midst of the fears and tears, and in wrath to remember mercy. God has always answered such supplication, filling each heart with His love, rekindling each soul with Fire from above.

Certainly it is high time that we prayed once more: "Wilt thou not revive us again, that thy people may rejoice in thee?" America has been a land of revivals. It was conceived in revival. Its foundations were laid by men who came out of the Puritan and Pietist revivals in England and on the Continent. In those early days, when hardship gave way to prosperity and men drifted away from God, the faithful few besought heaven and God sent the Great Awakening through the terrific preaching of Jonathan Edwards and the seraphic evangelism of George Whitefield. Spirituality flourished, the churches filled, and there was a preacher for every two thousand of our three million people.

But along came the French and Indian wars and the Revolution and brought the usual spiritual setback. Infidelity raised its head: Bolingbroke poisoned England; Voltaire corrupted France. Thomas Paine spread the deadly virus in America, until, as it has been said, "Our people had discovered that there could be a church without a pope, a land without a king and were on the point of deciding that there could be a world without a God." But, once again, the godly remnant prayed; God's people humbled themselves, and sought His face and turned from their wicked ways, and God heard from heaven, forgave their sin and healed their land. He answered with the Great Revival of 1800; shook Yale with Timothy Dwight; raised up Asbury and McKendree and James McGready, the Baptists in Kentucky, Peter Cartwright and the Methodist camp meetings. He followed it with wave after wave under Nettleton, Knapp and Finney.

The Great Revival lasted until 1842. Then prosperity set in again. Many thought the Golden Age had arrived. But, instead, came the Great Panic in 1857: banks failed, business closed its doors, railroads went into bankruptcy, everything came to a standstill. Once again, God had His pinch of salt in the earth. Believers prayed, "*Revive us again*," and, in answer, the Fulton Street prayer meetings set off a wave of prayer meetings all over the country that crossed the ocean and swept multitudes into the Kingdom of God. But war followed upon the heels of revival, and the blood of brothers flowed across the Mason and Dixon's Line; the Civil War debauched and demoralized the country, but the Lord heard His people again and raised up Dwight L. Moody. He defeated the devil with the Pentecostal power poured upon this rugged shoe salesman from Boston and followed His victory with Torrey and Chapman and Sunday. Then came another avalanche of blood and tears in 1914. Once again, the land has been corrupted and has had a moral and spiritual setback. BUT THIS TIME THERE HAS BEEN NO REVIVAL. The same conditions prevail today on a larger and worse scale than existed before the Great Revival. Then France had corrupted the world with atheism; today it is Russia. Then it was Hume and Voltaire and Tom Paine; today it is a motley mob of would-be intellectuals who follow in their train, not nearly as brilliant but a numerous aggregation of fools who rush in where angels fear to tread. Once again, the land has had a taste of prosperity and, as usual, has gone crazy. We live in a steam-heated, warm-bath era, more interested in the Here and Now than in preparing for the By and By. Instead of fleeing the City of Destruction, we are out to clean it up.

Surely today, the faithful few need to plead with the prayer of our forefathers, "Wilt thou not revive us again?" But, alas, little interest is shown by the Church in the need or possibility of revival. Since the World War, evangelism has become more and more unpopular. Prayer meetings have been supplanted by pep meetings. The social Gospel, religious education and training in Kingdom work have become the watchwords of the denominations. Revivals have fallen into disrepute, partly because of erratic, money-grabbing evangelists, but more because the Church is now trying to do by professionalism and propaganda what once she did by power and prayer and the preaching of Christ crucified.

Broadly speaking, the professing Church is divided into three groups: the Modernists, who have exchanged substance for shadow, preaching a denatured Gospel with the supernatural extracted, spraying with the rose water of a false optimism an ungodly world, vainly calling the righteous to repentance; the Denominationalists, who too often have forgotten the Person in zeal over a Program, lost in an ocean of statistics, born in revival fires, but now living in smoke; the Fundamentalists, most of whom are doctrinally sound, but many of whom are so busy castigating the leaven of the Sadducees that they themselves are smitten with the leaven of the Pharisees. Only a real revival can meet such a situation.

Will we have another revival? Yes, if the Lord tarries, and provided we meet the conditions. There is nothing accidental, hit-or-miss, magical about revivals. We have all the elements of revival in the words of the Psalmist, "*Wilt thou not revive us again: that thy people may rejoice in thee?*"

First, we have the Revival Prayer, for the verse is a supplication. A revival is a work of God, it cannot be stirred up by efforts of the flesh. It is not by might nor by power but by His Spirit. Church experts have planned dozens of ways to break up the Rip van Winkle slumbers of the saints and breathe into Sardis the breath of life. We have heard the slogan, "Every pastor his own evangelist." There have been house-to-house evangelism and Sunday-school evangelism, and many other diverse kinds of evangelism have been planned and practiced. Bernard Shaw said, "Americans have the best filing systems in the world,—but no American can ever find a letter!" So we have the best plans for revival in the world—but no revival!

Here, as elsewhere, "you can do more than pray after you have prayed, but you cannot do more than pray until you have prayed." Our prayer must be, "*Turn thou us unto thee, O Lord, and we shall be turned; renew our days as of old*" (Lamentations 5: 21). We are never truly turned to God until God turns us. It is His supernatural work, but the fact that men have prayed for revival and received it proves that God will turn His people in answer to fervent, effectual prayer.

Next, we have the Revival People, the people who are to be revived: "*Wilt thou not revive US again: that THY PEOPLE may rejoice in thee?*" A revival is God's work among God's people and we shall have revival when God's people pay the price. When born-again believers stop petty bickerings over nonessentials and go to their knees in old-fashioned, beseeching prayer we shall have revival. When Christians wear out more carpets around family altars than around dressing tables we shall have revival. When fathers stay home from the club, and mothers from bridge, and the children from the dance, and the car is left in the garage long enough to cool, and the radio is shut off long enough to tune in on God, we shall have revival. When Jacob buries his false gods under the oaks at Shechem, and Achan's wedge of gold is laid out before the Lord, we shall have revival. When preachers seek fresh anointing of Pentecostal fire, cut out pulpit essays and preach from the Bible with the power of the Holy Ghost sent down from heaven, we shall have revival. When churches quit trying to hold together by picnics and programs and get back from one discord to "*one accord*" and from the supper room to the Upper Room, we shall have revival. When backslidden Christians seek the lost joy of salvation, the upholding of

God's free Spirit, then transgressors shall be taught God's ways and sinners shall be converted.

There must be conviction of sin in the Church, confession of sin by the Church, conversion from the self-life to the Christ-life, for only when we are converted can we strengthen the brethren. There must be absolute surrender to God's will, fresh filling of the Spirit and a new walk in holiness, without which no man shall see the Lord. I do not know what form the next revival will take, but I do know that it will require an unusual charge of Divine Dynamite to blast out the smug complacency of this generation. Perhaps God may raise up another Finney, some human firebrand upon whom the mantle of the prophets has fallen, who shall come forth from the solitude, bringing a flaming message saturated with Power; who shall preach sin and redemption, judgment and repentance, those grand old themes of another day, when men did not play at preaching and sinners fell from their seats before the mighty two-edged Sword!

AGAIN, we have in our verse the REVIVAL PRODUCT —Joy: "*Wilt thou not revive us again: that thy people MAY REJOICE in thee?*" Habakkuk prayed, "*O Lord, revive thy work in the midst of the years,*" and ended his book rejoicing in the God of his salvation. Revival brings rejoicing. When Christians pass from sentence prayers to learn prevailing supplication; when God's people go back to Bethel and dwell there; when the Bible becomes more important than bridge, and the house of God more attractive than the theatre,—rejoicing is sure to follow. If ever God's people needed to rejoice, it is today. The amens and hallelujahs have gone from most churches. There has been substituted in some the artificial enthusiasm of human "pep," more suitable to a football game—a fake and counterfeit joy by which dying churches try to whistle their way past the graveyard. Sunday morning dignity, in other places, has supplanted supernatural delight, the saintly have given way to the sanctimonious. We cannot really sing, " Hallelujah, Thine the glory " until first we have truly sung, " *Revive us again.*" Only real revival can restore lost joy. It is said that in 1799, if one passed through the Northwest, he could hear on every side only swearing and obscenity, the songs of drunkards, the blasphemy of infidels in every village and hamlet. But in 1801 one could hear on every hand the Gospel being preached to multitudes, songs of praise to God all along the highways, prayers in the woods and groves. The Great Revival had come! If this land is to be spared wreck and ruin, there must be another such visitation of God among His people: a visitation in revival.

Notice, finally, in our verse the Revival Purpose—rejoicing in the Lord: " *Wilt thou not revive us again: that thy people may rejoice IN THEE?* " Not that God's people may rejoice in their big preacher or their great church, nor even in additions to their church; not that they may rejoice in denominational pride, nor in the report they sent to headquarters, nor even in how many demons were cast out. God is the One Object of our rejoicing. Any revival that does not center in the Lord, that does not exalt and magnify Him, that does not draw Christians to know the Lord Jesus Christ better and sinners to receive Him is a false revival. When our expectation is from Him, our joy will be in Him. And any revival that finds its climax anywhere but at His feet is not a Scriptural revival.

God help us to get low in the dust and pray like our forefathers, " *Wilt thou not revive us again: that thy people may rejoice in thee?* "

IV

OLD-TIME RELIGION

ROM the modern much-ado-about-nothing I often escape along the lanes of memory to the little country church of boyhood days. In reverie I sit once more beside my father in the amen corner during the midsummer "big meeting." They sing, "Amazing Grace" and "Brethren, We Have Met to Worship" and other songs which modern mortals are too proud to sing. There is an "experience meeting," where tears are shed and amens uttered, for emotion has not yet been outlawed in religion. There is a powerful sermon, perhaps long and loud; but if the preacher does not have the elegance of Apollos, he does have the conviction of Aquila; there are no dainty references to Spinoza and Schopenhauer, with a dash of Emerson and an epigram from Epictetus; God is Almighty, Jesus died for us, sin is black, judgment certain, eternity long, and we have souls to save—that is the message.

We sing, "Come, Ye Sinners, Poor and Needy," and they come, crowding the "mourners' bench." There are happy conversions, and if some sister breaks into a shout it is not the crowning disgrace of the season. Eventually, we all get home sometime in the early afternoon, feeling that it was good to have been at the house of the Lord.

Much water has run under the bridge since those plainer days. When occasion grants me to stroll among the simple graves of the humble folk who lived and laboured then, I feel no pity that they passed away before the pandemonium of Modernism broke loose. I have no desire to tell them what they missed by being born so soon. I fear that, should I point out the advantages of our speed, they might ask: "But what's the use? You are going nowhere!" If I brought up the wonders of radio, they might remind me, "But what have you to broadcast?" And I am sure I should feel naught but humiliation, could one of these fervid souls drop into the average church for an up-to-date, efficiency pep meeting. What a dour time I should have translating for him the new vernacular of the Church, borrowed from the world, when he had always thought religiously in the old phraseology born of the Word!

We would not paint around these old-time saints any brighter halo than really was theirs. We make due allowance for some ignorance, for undue sectarian pride, for many grievous faults better left untold. But if they did not always get the right explanation of their Scripture, they generally fell upon an application for it. If they did not always understand clearly just *what* God is, they did know *that* He is and that He is the rewarder of them that diligently seek Him. They may not have made religion their business at all times, but neither did they make business their religion as their children have done. What they lacked in organizing for God they made up in agonizing with God—and Jacob agonizing at Jabbok was accomplishing more than Jacob systematizing his gift for Esau. Some of these midsummer converts may have begun in a revival fire only to live the rest of their lives in the smoke, but that is not the fault of the fire nor of the revival; and it is better to be even "*smoking flax*" than never to have known the flame.

It is becoming more and more difficult for the present to pity the past. In the debacle of this Punch-and-Judy civilization some are beginning to discover that the faith of our fathers is not the back-number proposition it is thought to be by those to whom a little learning has become, indeed, a dangerous thing. The trail "from protoplasm to perfection" has run out in a wilderness.

But my heart is happy that God has made a provision for us in these perilous times.

"'Tis the old-time religion,
And it's good enough for me."

That simple ditty of other days had several verses such as "It was good for the Hebrew children," "It was good for the prophet Daniel," "It was good for Paul and Silas"; and we sang them in the unquestioning faith that took the Bible exactly for what it said in black and white. Higher criticism, reducing the Hebrew children to folklore, Daniel to an apocalyptic puzzle, and the Philippian incident to highly-coloured exaggeration, had not invaded those lowly hill folk. Children listened in wide-eyed wonder to the stories of these mighty men of old and professor-cynics had not as yet been imported to teach, at public expense, that our Bible beliefs were only the projection of our childish trust in fairies and Santa Claus.

We must either take the Book for what it says or leave it alone. Who are we to say that Almighty God did not specially manifest Himself in these early ages through men to whom our Lord referred in His messages again and again? What a futile theism is that which laughs at our conception of God as "an Oriental monarch" and then proceeds to imprison the Creator within His own laws! If He can make

His laws, He can overrule them. If He can make fire and men, why should I doubt that He can bring men through fire without burning? If He can create lions, He can control them. If He can break open buildings by earthquakes for other reasons, could He not do so in answer to prayer? So I can still sing with the old home church of Paul and Daniel and the Hebrew children. And that old-time religion is good enough for me—yes, too good for me, for I did not deserve it; it was His grace that made it mine!

We sang also in those other days, " It was good for our fathers," and " It was good for our mothers." I think of my own father, frail in body but strong in spirit, whom pleasure trips and picnics never carried away on Sundays from the place where prayer was wont to be made; the preacher's friend, his home the headquarters for all visiting ministers; the man to whom the neighbours came with their problems. Family prayers he never neglected and though often they were tedious for a restless youngster—little boys' knees sometimes grow tired in an incredibly short while—they wove a gentle influence which the years can never break. That was before the family had been " let out by auto and the world let in by radio." In later years, whenever I returned from here and there, I could always expect to see him standing beside the little old Ford at the small-town depot. I have missed his standing in that old familiar place for quite a while, but he waits elsewhere, for his was the old-time religion, and it pledges our reunion. Just before he fell asleep, he sang confidently, with failing breath:

" Jesus paid it all,
All to Him I owe;
Sin had left a crimson stain,
He washed it white as snow."

And that is the heart of the old-time religion!

The same holds true of a plain old mother, not very emotional or demonstrative, but, with childlike confidence, content to trust and obey. These old-fashioned mothers found in sweet, simple faith in Christ a satisfaction which modern sophisticates never know. One is reminded of the sick person who, when told by the physician, "You'll have to trust in God," answered despairingly, "Has it come to that?" Trusting in God is a sort of last desperate resort with some of us, to be taken only when everything else has failed. Why do we not trust Him at the outset instead of arriving there by a painful process of elimination? It is the old, old truth of Matthew 11: 25 and I Corinthians 1: 18–31; so many of us must poison ourselves with the world's prescriptions, and waste our days in futile quests on other trails, before we will humble ourselves to enter in at the strait gate, return to the old paths and find rest unto our souls. We might as well begin with the old-time religion of our mothers. Enough fools have tried all other roads in vain to save us the trouble if we can profit from their examples.

We sang also, concerning this old-time faith, "It makes me love everybody." We live in an age that likes to call itself cynical, nonchalant, "hard-boiled"—which is only another way of saying half-baked, like Ephraim, who was "a cake not turned." There is a cold callousness, an unfeeling heartlessness everywhere in these latter days, when men are "without natural affection." It sends a shiver through tender hearts and we wish that men had less smartness and more sympathy.

Now and then I preach in a Negro church. I enjoy that sense of affection and sympathy and fellowship which puts us white people to shame. They seem to think more of each other, there is a deep mutual understanding, a harmony which finds expression in the appealing unison of the spirituals they sing. I get hungry for that among my own people when I strike a church that seems more interested in being citified than sanctified. I am sure that one reason for so many suicides is that men find so little understanding and sympathy in a world of " every man for himself " that they grow desperate over burdens they need to share.

The old-time religion does make us love everybody. Paul uses often the phrase " faith in Christ Jesus and love to all the saints." They go together, for " he that loveth not his brother whom he hath seen, how can he love God whom he hath not seen? " We ministers love to preach to people, but often I wonder, do we love the people to whom we preach? There is a fellowship among believers who are walking in the light (I John 1: 7), a common understanding and sympathy which is utterly distinct from any other on earth. Civic clubs, social clubs, secret orders, leagues and brotherhoods of the world can never approach it, for it is a supernatural communion, a fellowship of eternity, in the world but not of it.

I have felt this unseen bond in the little church of my boyhood. We certainly were a plain-looking lot. It was a shabby church house, the preacher was plain, the organ wheezy and the music off key. But there was something that reminded one of the Upper Room and the " *one accord* " and " *all things common.*" We forgot our earthly limitations and felt ourselves to be heirs of God and joint heirs with Christ; the temporal faded and the eternal became real; we were burdened for lost sinners who were missing such a happy experience, and we loved to kneel around the mercy seat and pray for " our neighbours and neighbours' children," as we expressed it. It was a precious fellowship with God, its Author, and the Bible, its charter, and Christ, its Surety, that nothing could ever dissolve. Now and then one of the company slipped away, only to make fairer the prospect of perfect communion around the throne of God. There was a peculiar attachment to each other, for we felt ourselves to be pilgrims together through a strange world to a better land, passengers for a port eternal.

No amount of eloquence in the pulpit and elegance in the pew can compensate for the old faith that makes us love everybody. For the lack of sympathy and affection this world has grown cold and dismal; and for the lack of Christian love believers and churches have become sounding brass and tinkling cymbals. Emotion has been outlawed; the devout have become merely the dignified; Christian fellowship has given way to a friendly sociability, such as one can find in any club; and a stiff and starched Pharisaism marks the sad state of many a modern Ephesus which has left its first love.

We sang something else about this old-time religion: "It will do when I am dying." Now the emphasis upon death and the hereafter has departed from most preaching. We are exhorted, "Get ready to live and you will be ready to die." Modernists ridicule the theology of Jonathan Edwards, and deathbed experiences are reckoned only the stock in trade of sensational traveling evangelists. But, for all that, we still die, and, apart from the revelation in the Word, man knows no more in this proud age concerning death and beyond than the crudest savage in the jungles. In the face of death we want some more substantial hope than mere academic speculation about "survival of personality." That has a very learned sound, but it gives scant solace when we stand at the bier where lies one who meant more than all else earthly to us. No wonder that bereaved hearts wearily reply to such pale comfort:

> "*Console if you will, I can bear it,*
> *'Tis a well-meant alms of breath;*
> *But not all the preaching since Adam*
> *Has made death other than death.*"

But the old-time faith has made death other than death, for now we see it in the light of Christ. He went before us, conquered the grave, returned again to tell us so, and appeared again in His glory to John at Patmos to declare that He held the keys of death (Revelation 1: 18). Why should I dread it, if He holds the keys? His Word is sufficient for me; I do not need to piece out His guarantee with " intimations of immortality " from natural arguments. He said so, and I believe Him.

We usually finished our song about the old-time religion by singing, " It will take us all to heaven." How the world has mocked that simple confidence and called us " celestial excursionists! " It is the fashion of the times to sneer at the mansions in the Father's house, but there are still many of us who believe that,

> "*There's a land that is fairer than day,*
> *And by faith I can see it afar.*"

I remember how as a tiny boy I used to swing beneath the big oak back home, looking far to the western sky line where the sun sank among the Blue Ridge Mountains, singing simple, old songs of heaven, " Jesus Will Be There," " When I Can Read My Title Clear," and others that breathed sweet confidence in a better life to come. There were later years when heaven was farther away than when I was a boy. But still later years have brought heaven near again, and I could swing there now and sing the old songs as confidently as before. To me, that fair city is not merely the creation of wishful thinking. Nor do I believe in it simply from such arguments as man can muster apart from revelation, although upon even those grounds I cannot think that God has no better thing for a human life than some cosmic waste basket. I believe because the Saviour declared it, and I believe that simple faith in Him will lead me there.

We had better get back to the old-time religion. To many it looks impossible, its claims are so absolute, its conditions so simple. But when men renounce their prejudices and accept its provisions, it works. So few try it because with us poor cynics seeing is believing, when the principle of faith is that believing is seeing.

This unhappy generation has worked itself into a strange temper. It is an age of suspicion. If a man does a good deed there must be a catch in it somewhere. The pious get little credit for right living—they have something up their sleeves! With every man out for himself, an eye on his neighbour, critical and defiant, feverishly maneuvering to outwit before he is outwitted, it is manifestly a poor mood in which to appreciate the childlike trust for which the faith of our fathers calls.

When the minister reads such a text as "*Except ye be converted, and become as little children, ye shall not enter into the kingdom of heaven,*" he can almost feel a reaction from the sophisticates before him: "Become as children! How far would I get being childlike in a day like this?"

But some of us who laughed at grandmother's religion and deemed it as passé as her nightcap and knitting needles are learning that we are not so clever. It is one of life's strange turns that scholars ransack libraries looking for wisdom, while, perhaps, the janitor has found it long ago. We have been stocking our heads with "loads of learned lumber," but we have failed to build stately mansions for our souls. We would do well to sit again in the little rustic church at "meeting time." Some of those old saints may have been rather austere and forbidding, but, if they were like monks, we are like monkeys, and we had better keep our dunce-caps for ourselves. They knew whence they came and where they were going; they did not trace their origins to sentient jelly nor their destinies to dreamless dust. They believed that they were more than "small, crawling masses of impure carbohydrates" headed for oblivion. What matters it if our words circle the globe in split seconds and we can open our fairs with a light impulse from a star, if we are only accidents and life is only a pitiful puzzle that cannot be put together?

We prided ourselves that we would live life in our own way. But a man cannot live in his own way; if he does not live God's way he is living the devil's way. Because we had learned a few new secrets about the cosmic engine we thought we did not need the Engineer! Verily, God has kept His precious things from the wise and prudent and revealed them unto babes. If we are to find rest unto our souls we must renounce our heady pride and seek the old paths we thought impossible, and trust Him Who is the heart of the old-time religion, which is not really old-time nor new-time, but timeless, from eternity to eternity.

V

"IS IT NOTHING TO YOU?"

"*Is it nothing to you?*"—LAMENTATIONS 1: 12.

THE Prophet Jeremiah was a sad and solitary man of God in the midst of a corrupt and sinful nation rushing on to ruin. His heart was broken by the wickedness of his generation. His soul was so burdened with the sins of his people that he has come down in history as "the weeping prophet." He wished that his head were waters and his eyes a fountain of tears, that he might weep day and night for the slain of the daughter of his people. Once he even cried unto God: "*Wilt thou be unto me as a liar, and as waters that fail?*" Once he tried to be silent and keep still, but God's Word was as a fire shut up in his bones and he was weary with forbearing and could not stay.

No doubt the other preachers considered Jeremiah to be a highly nervous sort, unduly excited over the times. Likely they told him, "Now, Jeremiah, you cannot convert the world anyway, so take it easy. Don't get worked up over what you cannot help—you may bring on a nervous collapse." As for the people, they may have thought him to be a well-meaning but overwrought good man, a calamity-howler, specializing in messages on hard times. I can imagine them saying, "Why can't he be normal like the other preachers and prophesy unto us smooth things, prophesy deceits, healing slightly the hurt of the daughter of the people, saying 'Peace,' when there is no peace?"

But Jeremiah was not that kind of preacher. Others might take it easy, but not he. Others might see prosperity around the corner; others might paint the clouds with sunshine; others might hail the coming brotherhood of man, but not he. He knew which way the wind was blowing; he saw the fingers of God writing the doom of Jerusalem in box-car letters across the sky. And as he looked out through tear-dimmed eyes upon the careless multitudes passing by, blind to danger, deaf to God and sure for judgment, he cried in the words of our text, "*Is it nothing to you?*"

We are living at this hour in the midst of a nation that bears all the characteristics of the times of Jeremiah. It would seem that if ever there was a time when men and women would be wide awake with a vivid sense of crisis and emergency, it would be today, when astounding world events tumble over each other in rapid succession, when governments crash and the foundations of society crumble and wars and rumours of wars rumble around the world. It would seem that a generation living on the edge of such a world-wide volcano could scarcely sleep at night for fear of the coming day.

But, on the contrary, the world rushes madly by as it did in the days of the weeping prophet. And if some faithful watchman of God does dare to sound the danger signal, modern prophets, busy with ethical programs and social gospels, brand him as a disturber of the peace. But, for all that, some of us cannot keep silent. His Word is as a fire shut up in our bones, and we are weary with forbearing and cannot stay. In the midst of world confusion we would cry to a generation of indifferent passers-by: "*Is it nothing to you?*"

Is it nothing to the people of this country that America, without leadership, is headed for destruction? It would seem that patriotism, if nothing else, would lead us to examine ourselves; it would seem that love of country would cause us to check up the reasons for our national emergency. But multitudes know little about what is wrong and care even less; millions drink and dance the time away at the modern feast of Belshazzar, while God writes on the wall. Others run after this politician and that with their promises and panaceas, the blind trying to follow the blind to a land of milk and honey. How many believe that our iniquities have separated us from our God, and that our sins have hid His face from us, so that He will not hear? How many are turning to God's plan for national recovery: "*If my people, which are called by my name, shall humble themselves, and pray, and seek my face, and turn from their wicked ways; then will I hear from heaven, and will forgive their sin, and will heal their land*"?

But we do not expect people at large to understand the cause and cure of the world's distress, for the god of this world hath blinded their minds. However, when we turn to the Church, the most humiliating scandal of the times is that still we must ask, "*Is it nothing to you?*"

One wonders whether Jeremiah would not first ask the preachers of today, "*Is it nothing to you?*" Our pulpits are filled with good, honest and trained men. Yet even in the ministry of today there is a burdening sense that we are not meeting the situation. Some are ground between the millstones of a daily routine of small duties, ecclesiastical Marthas cumbered with much serving and with no time to sit at the feet of the Lord, so busy with the good that there is not time for the best. Others have gone after a social gospel which, indeed, looks like the very thing for such an hour, but is really a substitution of preaching of rose water for repentance. We ministers are not sufficiently stricken with a sense of crisis, not only in the distress around us, but in the dearth within us—the poverty of our own souls. We hold our conferences, we agree that something ought to be done, that we need more power, but we soon move on to another subject—we are not "*grieved for the affliction of Joseph.*" If God does raise up here and there a prophet with the spirit of Jeremiah, he is dubbed a pessimist. We peddle a cheap, easy, Pollyanna optimism, declaring that "God's in His heaven, all's right with the world," when we need to go to our knees for a fresh anointing of power, then to stand in the gate and declare, "All is not well with the world, prepare to meet thy God!"

There is a pleasant teaching today that all we need is just to move along with a simple moment-by-moment faith. That is the normal experience, but special emergencies demand special experiences with God and unusual infillings of power. There are times when Jacob, being left alone, must wrestle at Jabbok. Our Lord lived in continuous dependence upon the Father but in crises He continued all night in prayer. There come times of holy desperation when, as others in the Gospels did, we must tear up roofs and climb sycamores and press through the crowds to get to Jesus for fresh blessings.

We marvel at the preaching of Savonarola and Whitefield and Edwards and Finney and Evans. If you ask, "Where do we have such preaching today?" we must ask, "Where do we have such men today who will seek through prayers and fastings till the Word of God becomes fire in their mouths and the people are consumed before them?" How many today are losing sleep for the wretchedness of the people and the weakness of their own hearts? Ought we not to pray like the early Church, "Lord, once again the rulers of earth are gathered against the Lord and the Christ. . . . *Grant unto thy servants that with all boldness they may speak thy word"?* Alas, it is nothing to us! The distress of the times and the dearth of our souls mean nothing. We can discuss them, then forget them—they are merely topics for shallow and superficial consideration.

Our Lord promised to fill to overflowing those who thirsted for the living water of the Spirit. But thirsting is something more than just wanting a drink of water, and our shallow desire for blessing today does not approach that burning thirst of souls who prayed through to mighty power with God and men in other days. We speculate about the difference between "baptism" and "filling" of the Spirit, but if we cared enough, we would forget argument and wait upon God until theology went up in doxology! It meant something to Christmas Evans when, being "convicted of a cold heart," he prayed until God mightily warmed his heart "like the breaking up of a hard winter." It meant something to John Livingston who prayed all night, and next day, a great audience being assembled, was so overcome with a sense of unworthiness that he started to run, but returned to preach two and one half hours, which resulted in the conversion of five hundred.

We turn to professing Christians at large to ask, *"Is it nothing to you?"* When dance halls are packed and theatres are crowded to the doors, while church members sit comfortably at home on prayer-meeting nights with their faces buried in a newspaper, we need not wonder that the Great Awakening has not come. While the devil packs the aisles of the show places of sin, ministers stand in near-vacant churches and preach their hearts out to wildernesses of wood. Church members sit in the movies and cry over the glycerine tears of a divorcee actress, or yell themselves hoarse at football matches; but on Sunday, while some man of God pleads for lost millions on foreign fields or for lost boys and girls in the very homes of the Church, the silence is so profound you would think it was the tomb of King Tut.

"*Is it nothing to you?*" Is it nothing that Christ came to save sinners and called you to be fishers of men? Is it nothing that you live for self and none beside, just as if Jesus had never lived, and as if He had never died? Is it nothing that every day, every hour, souls leap into eternity that you might have rescued had you been awake? Say not ye, "There are yet four months till harvest." "*The fields are white already to harvest!*"

Sometime ago I received a letter from a missionary friend in Manchuria. Out there it was forty below zero and he had been out on a preaching trip riding in a third-class car with ice freezing on the floor, so cold that the engines had to be changed three times. Yet they met there at daybreak for prayer meetings and he asked how many of us would meet at such an hour in such a climate! Do you wonder that a spirit of revival is there and that there is none here?

Not long ago I sat at lunch near a group of stamp collectors. I do not understand the language of philately, but I know they were tremendously enthusiastic and all afire with a fervour for collecting stamps. I sat there convicted, and thought, "My God, I am a collector of souls for Thee! '*He that gathereth not with me scattereth abroad*'; '*Thou shalt catch men'*—that means me. And yet I am not as excited about collecting jewels for God as these people are rummaging around for postage stamps!"

"In the strength of the Lord let me labour and pray,
Let me watch as a winner of souls,
That bright stars may be mine in the glorious day,
When His praise like the sea billows rolls.

"Will there be any stars, any stars in my crown,
When at evening the sun goeth down,
When I wake with the blest in the mansions of rest,
Will there be any stars in my crown?"

Mr. Moody used to tell of a missionary conference where an aged and broken-down missionary home from India fainted while making a passionate plea for India. When he recovered in another room he demanded to go back and finish his speech, and back he went and cried to the audience, "If no one else will go to India, I will go back! If I cannot live for India, I will die for India!" There was a man who cared!

My Christian friends, is it nothing to you? Is a lost world nothing to you? Is the coldness of your own heart nothing to you? In the past, when conditions such as these settled upon the world, God's people who cared assembled themselves in agonizing prayer for revival, and, in due time, the windows of heaven were opened. Today in our churches we are frantically trying to keep all the wheels going around instead of making fresh connection with the Source of power. We have built a vast machine and now we feel that it must be kept running by some kind of power, human power if not divine. We think that we must have so many meetings, that so many sermons must be preached, so many committees must meet, so many salaries must be paid, so much money must be raised. We dare not let up for a day, for fear that we shall be bankrupt and the denominational pride be scandalized. Somehow or other, the schedule must be kept!

It might be confusing for the moment, but it would be better to call off half the meetings, to give the committees a vacation, and even to miss several Sunday services, while preacher and people caught their breath, got on their knees, and prayed down a fresh Pentecost. To be sure, it would create a stir in town and people would be gathered in huddles, wondering why the churches failed to open on schedule time; but that would be better than running on time while the crowds go by and hardly know that anything is going on inside the churches. I do not think we would miss many meetings, but if we did, and stayed on our knees and confessed and prayed until we received fresh power from above, one meeting after that would be worth a hundred before, and we would soon be out of debt, for when people first give themselves to the Lord, like the Macedonians, the money follows.

We have sunk into a rut and a routine. There is no divine urgency, no sense of crisis, no staggering burden of the awfulness of our times and the poverty of our own souls. To be sure, we have been "snowed under" with propaganda about the emergency in our denominations, but that is a side issue to which we have given first place. If the emphasis had been placed on the crisis of a lost world and a powerless Church, and the need for fresh filling of the Spirit, the real needs of every denomination would be met as a secondary by-product. We are not burdened with the real need. It is nothing to us.

I cannot but ask the sinner, too, "*Is it nothing to you?*" Is it nothing to you that you live in the closing days of the age, that the wrath of God abideth on you, that you are condemned already? Does it not matter that Christ died for you, that He gave His life a ransom for many, that He became poor that you through His poverty might be made rich?

Not only is there no sense of crisis in the country and in the Church, but there is no sense of emergency among the unsaved, because men have lost consciousness of the awfulness of sin, of the certainty of judgment and the horror of hell. In other days, when men realized that sin was black and life was short and judgment certain and eternity long, when preachers, knowing the terror of the Lord, persuaded men, warning them that it was a fearful thing to fall into the hands of the living God Who is a consuming fire—in those days sinners fell on their faces and cried, "*What must I do to be saved?*" Salvation meant something then. Today the eternal realities of a holy God and of sin and hell and judgment are phrases of another day. Conversion is not what once it was; people march glibly down the aisles to "join church" upon shallow and superficial "decisions for Christ." One wonders whether men who never have realized the bitterness of conviction can fully realize the blessedness of conversion.

Let me remind you that in the midst of all our problems, national, Church, and individual, stands Christ Himself saying, "*Ye will not come to me, that ye might have life.*" The greater question really is, "Is HE nothing to you?" "*Is IT nothing to you?*"—that is the SIN-QUESTION, but the answer to the sin-question is the SON-QUESTION.

HE is the answer to IT. He is the solution of every problem, the key to every situation.

May God awaken this nation, the Church and the lost to the call of the ancient prophet, "*Is it nothing to you?*" that we may look unto Him Who alone can meet our need.

VI

"HE IS BESIDE HIMSELF"

"He is beside himself."—MARK 3: 21.

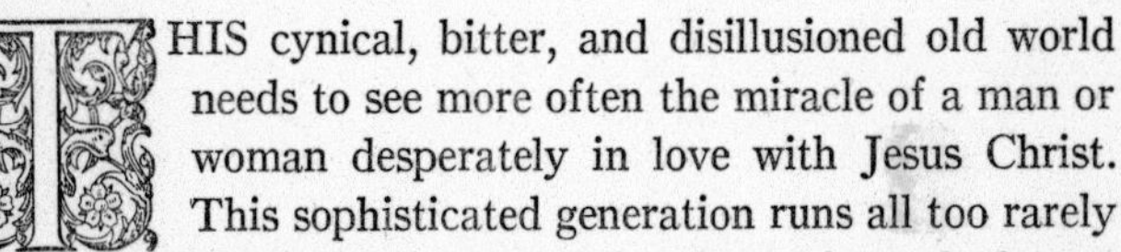

HIS cynical, bitter, and disillusioned old world needs to see more often the miracle of a man or woman desperately in love with Jesus Christ. This sophisticated generation runs all too rarely into the phenomenon of a human torch passionately happy to be the fuel of the Flame of God. Such human firebrands as these sweep through the dead, dull world around them making ordinary Christianity look drearily tame and commonplace. To meet such a soul is like finding a visitor from another planet—as indeed it is meeting an ambassador from another realm, one whose citizenship is in heaven.

The eyes of the Lord run to and fro throughout the earth looking for one person who will really consent to burn up for God. We sing about it, preach about it, pray about it; but few are the reckless souls who actually will become fools for Christ's sake, who will love not their lives to the death, and count them not dear, who gladly will fling themselves with holy abandon at the feet of their Lord. We sing:

"To the old rugged Cross I will ever be true,
Its shame and reproach gladly bear."

But we leave the reproach in the hymn book; to be counted the scum of the earth and the offscouring of all things is too much for us who love all too well to keep up with the Joneses. Ours is a respectable, comfortable faith; we will consent to attend a missionary meeting and listen to some scarred veteran tell of enduring hardship in a distant land. We may even shed a sympathizing tear and contribute gladly to let another perform the task. But for you or me to be consumed with the zeal of God's house until relatives shall grow solicitous about our mental state as did the friends of our Lord, or to stir up the gift of God within us until smouldering coals shall blaze into Heavenly Flame, and Festus complain that we are mad—ah, we much prefer our own comfort! "*He is beside himself*" (Mark 3: 21). They said it of our Lord. "*Thou art beside thyself*" (Acts 26: 24). They said it of Paul. "*Whether we be beside ourselves, it is to God*" (II Corinthians 5: 13). They will say it of us if we walk in their steps. (And why shouldn't we be "*beside ourselves*"? We are nothing *in* ourselves!)

There are not two gospels, one for missionaries and martyrs, the other for those who name the name of Christ but let Him bear the Cross alone while they themselves go free. In the beginning of the Church it was not only the apostles who were beside themselves. That entire first fellowship of saints lived so truly like a colony of heaven, not conformed to the world but transformed, that the world hounded them and branded them as the wildest of fanatics. No wonder they shook the world! Such people have always been well-nigh irresistible. What can stand before a blood-washed, fire-baptized throng, rejoicing to be counted worthy to suffer for Jesus' name?

It is possible to know such a consuming love for Jesus Christ that one is lifted to a holy abandon and a heavenly recklessness and is hilariously immune to this world's fears and fevers. There are few men and women who have not been at some time in their lives so desperately in love with someone that they were beside themselves and often almost irrational in their exhilaration. If the love of man for woman can so intoxicate us, is it not to our everlasting shame that our hearts can be so unresponsive toward Christ Jesus, Lover of our souls? Must He not stand among us today, grieved at the hardness of our hearts, and say as He did long ago: *"I have somewhat against thee, because thou hast left thy first love"*?

If we loved Him desperately, if we loved Him so passionately that all other loves were as hatred, if we loved Him as He deserves to be loved, would not our hearts rise above the circumstances and conditions of this dull world? Have you not seen young lovers so absorbed in each other that they were oblivious to all else? If we loved Him truly, would we not be unmindful of most things that concern and worry us now? And have you not noticed also how love makes the lover kindly disposed toward everyone except that one who would steal the affections? If we loved our Lord with the whole heart, we would love all men and hate only him who would break our communion, Satan, the archenemy of our souls.

We have toned down the first-century Christian fervour because it makes our insipid church life look pitiful in comparison. Scholars have endeavoured to establish that the characteristics of those early saints were not meant to be sustained down through the centuries—that the first flaming fervour was a sort of double portion to get the Church off to a good start!

But who can believe that God meant for His people to begin at a high pitch and then slip gradually off key through the ages as though He Who began such a good work were unable to continue it? Who dares to charge Almighty God with such unwisdom that would begin a work by raising high hopes which later He would not fulfill? Those early Christians were no favourites of God, enabled to live lives which never can be duplicated again. They simply paid the price, but we lazily excuse ourselves today by confining such power to the apostolic age, with the threadbare conclusion that "the day of miracles has passed." The day of miracles has not passed; the day of faith, miraculous faith, largely has passed!

The truth is that the early Christians were a despised sect, for the most part from the poorer and plainer classes, desperately in love with Christ and utterly beside themselves in their devotion to Him. They did not transform the world—they transcended it. It was only in later years, when Constantine made Christian profession easy and the Church ceased looking for the Lord to return and began trying to build heaven on earth, that Christians became "reasonable" and the world could live comfortably with them.

Let it not be forgotten that a twice-born and Spirit-filled Christian is always a contradiction to this old world. He crosses it at every point. From the day that he is born again, until he passes on to be with the Lord, he pulls against the current of a world forever going the other way. If he allows it, men will tone him down, steal the joy of his salvation, reduce him to the dreary level of the average. The real firebrand is distressing to the devil, and when a wide-awake believer comes along, taking the Gospel seriously, we can expect sinister maneuvering for his downfall. Alas, Satan receives no little aid from church members themselves in this matter, for most church folk dislike having their Laodicean complacency upset by those who insist on walking by faith and not by sight. There are many who raise their eyebrows and shrug their shoulders and bid the flaming zealot, "*Be not righteous over much!*"

There is no denying that the present-day world set-up is as definitely of the prince of darkness as was the world of the New Testament, yes, even more so as the return of the Lord draws near. It cannot be argued that we are excused from living such otherworldly lives as did the early Christians because the world has now become more Christian and the contrast is therefore not so pronounced. The contrast is *more* pronounced nowadays than ever whenever a Christian really dares to live the transformed and not the conformed life. Whosoever will be the friend of the world is the enemy of God (cf. James 4: 4); and, the time being short, we should live accordingly (I Corinthians 7: 29–31). "Propriety" and formalism and dim, religious atmosphere have smothered the fire, and repressed Christians huddle over coals that need to be fanned into flame by the stirring up of the Gift of God within us. With some happy exceptions, too often we shall find the brightest flame in some humble church on a back street—which is quite in keeping with the early assemblies—and even there sometimes extravagances reveal that Satan, never-sleeping, is attending as an angel of light.

Living beside oneself is no new or fanciful thing. Men have lost themselves in lesser causes than Christ and the Gospel. Men have lost themselves again and again in a flaming devotion to art or literature or scientific research or exploration. The devil has shown us the opposite of devotion to Christ in the reckless abandon of Communists and anarchists to their causes. Patriotism numbers by the millions those who have flung themselves into the jaws of death for love of country. But only the man who is beside himself for the love of Christ has truly lost his life to find it.

Most of us never get beyond interest—and mild interest at that—in eternal issues. We need not wonder that revival fails to sweep the world, that we make slight impression upon this wretched generation. Men are not moved by merely interested people. It took Pentecost to stir Jerusalem, and it takes the terrific dynamic of the Holy Ghost, through flaming witnesses, to make this sleeping world sit up and listen to the wonderful works of God. If we who claim to know and love the Lord display but casual interest in the Prince of Glory, need we wonder that a cynical world sees no reason to be wrought up about the saving of the soul?

But why is our love for Christ so cold, and what may we do about it? I fear that many who name His name never really have met Him in conversion. I am convinced that we invite many church members forward for consecration who need first to be saved. And after conversion there must be communion. Love increases as we associate with the person loved. This we do with Christ through the Spirit by prayer and the Word. And by all means remember that oft-forgotten road of obedience: "*He that hath my commandments, and keepeth them, he it is that loveth me: and he that loveth me shall be loved of my Father, and I will love him, and will manifest myself to him*" (John 14: 21). We cannot love the Lord with human love, but only with the love of God, God's own love, which is shed abroad in our hearts by the Holy Spirit. But that heart must be hungry for His love, and willing, and obedient. And as His love is received by faith, it is expressed in love for the brethren, thereby proving that we have passed from death to life; and that love flows out in love for the lost whom God so loved that He gave His only begotten Son.

Yes, it is the apostolic fervour of men and women desperately in love with Jesus Christ that this calloused world needs to witness today. Nowhere has the devil been more successful than in toning down this early zeal to a pale churchly religiousness. Some would have us believe that people are too intelligent nowadays to return to camp-meeting emotionalism. Well, this is certainly a poor time to credit anything to increased intelligence! Besides, that theory does not account for the fact that the same intelligent people who sit unmoved at church can be beside themselves in hours of frenzy at a football game or a political mass meeting. No, there is still plenty of fervour in the land, but not about the Lord!

The happiest person on earth is a young Christian ablaze with the fire of a new faith before he has met too many theologians! For every man born blind who receives his sight, the devil has fifty Pharisees ready to cool his ardour. The saddest sight I know is a Bible scholar or preacher (often a fundamentalist) who has left somewhere among his books the first love of his Christian youth. Better blaze through with more zeal than knowledge than to lose the calliope notes of early faith in a maze of contradictory commentaries and expositions! Better crash through believing too much than too little. Methinks God must prefer a too exuberant faith that He must check a little (if such is possible) to a pale orthodoxy that says the words but really does not believe them.

God give us some fervid souls who will let no one quench the Spirit within them!

VII

THE LOST AXE HEAD

THERE is recorded in the account of Elisha's ministry an interesting little story with great applications (II Kings 6: 1-7).

Elisha had gathered around him a little school of prophets, a sort of traveling theological seminary. But these preachers built their own hall; they did not expect a marble mansion, they were content with rough and humble quarters. As Matthew Henry quaintly puts it: " It becomes the sons of the prophets who profess to look for great things in the other world to be content with mean things in this." These prophets, probably not being able to hire labourers, set out, one at least with a borrowed axe, to construct their own dwelling place. Thus prophecy went hand in hand with poverty as it has often done.

The story that follows is simple. One went to work probably with a vehemence characteristic of many preachers doing manual labour when not accustomed to it. The axe head flew off and into the water. The young prophet was distressed over the loss of his borrowed axe head, but when he showed Elisha the place where it fell a stick of wood was cast into the water and the iron did swim.

Many of the Lord's workmen today have lost the axe head of power. They have lost the joy of salvation, they have not the upholding of God's Spirit. The axe head of the

Spirit's unction has fallen into the waters of worldliness, ponds of indifference, swamps of sluggishness. They have ability, training, sincerity, earnestness, but they are chopping with the handle. They stand before a demonized world powerless, and it must be said of them, as it was said of the disciples before the devil-possessed boy, "*And they could not*" (Mark 9: 18). The pitiful tragedy of the lost axe heads in the churches today!

Observe, first, that this axe head was borrowed. The believer's power for service is from God, he has nothing he did not receive. He may study, have personality, enthusiasm, but the axe head is borrowed. The man who had callers at midnight begged his neighbour, "*LEND me three loaves*" (Luke 11: 5), and when we face our friends who come to us for spiritual food and have nothing to set before them, we must get it from God. God's mighty workmen of the past wrought with borrowed axes, not by might nor power, but by His Spirit. Our churches today are filled with workers offering strange fire, as did Nadab and Abihu, and trying to do the work of God with human power, fervent in spirit, but not filled with the Spirit. Chopping with only the handle!

Consider, next, that this workman lost his axe head. The tragedy of lost power! Was there a time when you could pray with liberty, teach with power, preach with freedom? Was there a time when you had influence with your children, and your neighbours had confidence in your testimony? And now you have lost the axe head; it has fallen into the water of business cares, pleasure, worldly living, evil habits, indifference or laziness. You are a castaway, on the sidetrack, disapproved. You are going through the same old motions of woodchopping, but it is all a vain show, for the power is not there—it is but form without force.

Notice that this young prophet was concerned over the loss of the axe head: "*Alas, master! for it was borrowed.*" Worst of all is to be powerless and not to know it. Samson wist not that the Lord was departed from him (Judges 16: 20). Sardis had a name to be alive, but was dead (Revelation 3: 1). Pitiful indeed are preachers and churches going through all the exercises of chopping, faithfully, earnestly, yet unaware that the axe head of God's anointing long since has gone!

Consider, again, that the prophet stopped chopping until the axe head was recovered. That was natural, but would to God that His workmen would stop hollow motions in His service until power be recovered. This man did not pick up a substitute, but we substitute enthusiasm and energy of the flesh for God's Spirit. Someone has said: "There is an abundance of energy in the Church today, but it is not conquering energy conscious of power, but feverish energy conscious of its impotence." Men work all the harder to hide their lack of power as sometimes the preacher pounds the pulpit all the harder when he has run out of something to say. But there is no sense in working doubly fast with the handle just to keep men from seeing that there is no axe head on it!

It might be embarrassing, but it would be profitable for all preachers, deacons, and church workers who are chopping with the handle to stop until they find their axe heads. There might be some commotion at churches next Sunday if all such powerless Christians did not put in their appearance, but it would drive home the truth that God's work must be done by God's people in God's Way. It is not what is done

FOR Him but BY Him that counts, and if we labour without Him, we might as well quit until we abide in Him, for only then do we bear fruit to His glory.

If anything needs complete revision and overhauling today, it is our so-called "Christian work." If the average church were put through a genuine house cleaning according to New Testament standards and reconstructed according to the Acts, most members might have difficulty in recognizing it next Sunday morning!

Elisha asked the distressed workman, "*Where fell it?*" The place to find lost power is where you lost it. If you have disobeyed God, go back there and confess it; you really cannot move further along until you pass that point, for wherever we get out of God's will, there our progress stops. You never can get past the place where you left God's plan for your life until you confess and are restored to fellowship. You may be active, but you only "mark time."

I read in this account, "*And he showed him the place.*" He knew where he lost the axe head. And you know where you lost power. Was it when you became engrossed in business? When you gave up praying and Bible reading? When you quit going to church? When the pleasures of the world enticed you astray or when malice or envy filled your heart? GO BACK THERE AND SHOW GOD THE PLACE! Confess that sin! Give up that habit! Restore that family altar! Be reconciled to that brother! Surrender that wedge of gold hidden in your tent! God is asking, "*Where fell it?* Where did you grieve the Spirit?" "*He that covereth his sins shall not prosper: but whoso confesseth and forsaketh them shall have mercy*" (Proverbs 28: 13). If you are not sure of the place, let God turn His searchlight upon it, He will show you where fell the axe head.

Thank God for the next point: " *And the iron did swim!* " When the stick was cast into the water, the impossible happened. Iron does not usually float in such a manner, but ours is the God of the impossible. Will God restore lost power and uphold with His free Spirit? Gladly, if we meet His conditions. There must be confession before God can cleanse and empower. When Peter is converted, he is able to strengthen the brethren and feed the sheep. When the lost joy is restored and the Spirit upholds, then transgressors are taught His ways and sinners converted unto Him.

Finally, we note that " *he put out his hand and took it.*" After sin is confessed, then faith receives the power restored. To ask and then fail to take is to add another sin, the sin of unbelief. " If we confess our sins, he is faithful and just to forgive us our sins, and to cleanse us from all unrighteousness " (I John 1: 9). To doubt our forgiveness and wallow in misery after sin has been confessed is to distrust His faithfulness.

Have you lost the axe head? Are you chopping with the handle? Please stop, until the power has been restored! It need not be long, only long enough to show God the place, to confess, receive, believe. And remember, then, that the axe head is yours not merely to display or boast about, but to use. His power is for witnessing and service. So keep on chopping wood!

VIII

PRESS THROUGH TO JESUS

THE Lord Jesus was on His way to the house of Jairus. A multitude of people thronged Him on every side. In the midst of the crowd was a poor woman who suffered from a threefold adversity. She had an incurable disease; she had spent all she had on physicians, and was worse instead of better; and she was ceremonially unclean.

In such a miserable condition she had become desperate. Something HAD to be done. She heard that Jesus was passing by. She resolved: "I must get through to Him. I cannot go on like this. I have tried the doctors, I have spent my money, I am dying by degrees. I must elbow my way into His presence. It is my last chance, it is do or die!"

So, human extremity became God's opportunity. The best thing that can happen to any of us is to be reduced to HOLY DESPERATION. It is only then that we press through to Jesus. So long as we have health and friends and money and a position, we do not feel any particular need of the Lord. Most of us, like Jacob, must be "*left alone*" at some Jabbok, with all earthly props knocked out, before we reach real power with God and men. At the breaking point of desperation we usually do one of two things: we commit suicide, or we get right with God.

Do you recall the four lepers at the gate of Samaria (II Kings 7: 3–9)? Behind them was the besieged city starving in famine; before them lay the besieging army of the Syrians. The lepers had come to desperation and they said one to another: "*WHY SIT WE HERE UNTIL WE DIE?*" They reasoned that if they sat still they would die; if they went into the city, they would starve. There was one other alternative, to go into the camp of the Syrians. "*If they save us alive, we shall live; and if they kill us, we shall but die,*" they reasoned. In other words: "We are going to die anyway. Why not take a chance and venture forward? It cannot be worse, and it may be better." So they entered the camp of the Syrians, to find them gone with all the spoils and bounty of the camp left at their disposal!

Many a soul has sat in the zero hour of desperation with despair back of him, despair around him and only one possible hope left,—a bold venture of faith straight ahead, apparently into the jaws of death. But out of that blackest hour he has risen, asking, "Why sit I here until I die?" and has marched straight ahead to find that God has gone before, defeated the enemy and left the spoils of victory to him who fares forth by faith to find them.

It may be a blessing sometimes to reach the bitter extremity where one would as soon be dead as to go on like that—out of such a crisis more than one has started to Jesus singing:

"I can but perish if I go;
I am resolved to try;
For if I stay away, I know
I must forever die."

In some such spirit this poor, wretched woman resolved to press through to Jesus. Desperation is not enough: she had FAITH. She believed that if she could get through to Jesus she would be healed. It may have been a very imperfect faith, but it is not the quality or the quantity of faith that matters most; it is the object of faith. If we believe enough to press through all obstacles and touch the hem of His garment we shall be blessed as though we had all the faith in the world. As a matter of fact, the woman had more faith than she thought. She came "*fearing and trembling,*" but our Lord said, "*Thy faith hath made thee whole.*" She got through to Jesus, and that is what matters! It is not great faith, but faith in a great Christ.

But, mind you, it was faith that PRESSED THROUGH TO JESUS. There is where we fail today. We let the crowd get between us and Him. We press through to some book or favourite teacher or doctrine, but we do not press through to Him. According to the Gospels, those who got the greatest blessings were those who went to greatest pains to get through to Jesus; for instance, the paralytic who was let down through the roof. There was another crowd, but this man had friends who were determined somehow to press into the presence of the Lord. There would be more miracles today if more of us dared tear up the roofs of the customary and conventional to reach Jesus.

There was Zacchæus, who also faced the problem of a crowd and solved it by climbing the sycamore. That was certainly an irregular thing for one so prominent and so unpopular as Zacchæus to do, but when a man wants to see the Lord seriously enough, nothing else matters. If we cared enough today to risk the scorn of this unbelieving world and climb sycamores in holy desperation, the story of our poor lives would read differently. Many saw Jesus on that day, but only Zacchæus had the Lord as his guest. Those who would know His greatest blessings must let nothing defeat them in their zeal to see the Saviour.

The Syrophenician woman was another who would not be put aside without the needed blessing. First she was answered with silence, and next with a withering remark that put her with the little dogs at the table. But she was desperate, there was awful need at home, and when we are desperate enough nothing will offend us.

Right here lies the trouble with the rich young ruler. He was not desperate. He was a fine young fellow who wanted to "do the right thing" and, along with his other attainments, he wanted to inherit eternal life. But he was not desperate and our Lord knew it. So He demanded that the young ruler cut loose from his possessions and burn all bridges behind him, for only so could he live with utter, absolute, reckless abandon. This he was not willing to do, which shows that he had never reached that spiritual extremity that cries, "*Why sit we here until we die?*" No man can truly follow the Christ until he is desperately committed to God alone. That does not mean that every rich man must give away his money, but it does mean that he must reach the point where he is as though he had none. Few ever do that, so it is hard for a rich man to enter the kingdom. So long as we lean with part of our weight on some resource other than the Lord, we can never know God's fullest blessing.

"Let our debts be what they may,
However great or small,
So soon as we have naught to pay,
Our Lord forgives us all;

'Tis perfect poverty alone that sets
The soul at large;
While we can call one mite our own
We have no full discharge."

Mind you, this woman was shy and timid. She was not in the habit of elbowing her way through the crowds. But when we are desperate enough, we will do anything to get through to relief. Our Lord said, "If any man thirst, let him come unto me and drink." We have never put enough emphasis upon that word, "thirst." Casually wanting a drink of water is not thirsting. When we really thirst, water MUST be had, and we will drive through any obstacle to get it if it is to be had. Christians do not drink of the Living Water of the Spirit because there is no burning, feverish, consuming thirst after God. We read about the fulness of the Spirit, hear about it, pay preachers to tell about it, but the average Christian is only mildly interested—the whole subject is simply one of those polite topics for pleasant after-dinner conversation. There is no driving, desperate sense of need such as drove this poor sick woman to press through to Jesus.

She not only pressed through; she TOUCHED Him. He asked, "*Who touched me?*" The disciples thought it a strange thing to ask. "In such a crowd with everybody pressing you, how can you ask, 'Who touched me?'" Ah, but there was only one who really TOUCHED Him that day. Many people jostled Him, crowded Him, thronged Him, but only one touched Him. It is so today. We go to church on Sunday, we crowd the Lord, we pay Him respect, but few, very few, ever really touch Him with a faith that lays hold of His divine virtue. And the reason is, that few have any desperate sense of need. We sit in church, we listen, but we are not overwhelmed with urgency and emergency. The whole matter is one we can take or leave. "Of course, it is all very splendid, but I can do without it." We are leaning on so many other things, we have not reached extremity. We are "*rich and increased with goods and HAVE NEED OF NOTHING.*" So, we do not touch Him, and, consequently, His virtue does not go out into our lives and we go away empty, while some poor, wretched soul, driven to desperation, simply touches the hem of His garment and is made whole.

How many things will get in the way when a soul starts to Jesus! The crowd hindered Zacchæus, and it hindered this poor woman. The crowd always hinders, for the multitudes today are not minded to touch Jesus, and they will laugh at the desperate soul who elbows through into His presence. Then, fear and doubt and weakness beset this poor, seeking soul. She might have reasoned: "What is the use? He won't notice me, a poor, hopeless woman. I might as well give up and go home to die."

And people can't see any sense in it. In this connection, there came some from the house of Jairus, saying, "*Thy daughter is dead: why troublest thou the Master any further?*" Men are so ready to give up and pronounce the case hopeless. But what did the Lord say? "*BE NOT AFRAID, ONLY BELIEVE!*" Never accept the verdict of man. "*Is anything too hard for the Lord?*" "*All things are possible to him that believeth!*"

Even the Church often gets in the way of a soul pressing through to Jesus. Remember how they who went before rebuked Bartimæus, that he should hold his peace? How often do those who travel with Jesus at least in profession discourage wayside beggars! Remember how the disciples rebuked those who brought little children to the Lord that He might bless them. But when the Lord saw it, He was much displeased, and so He is today when we crowd out with our formality and indifference the needy, desperate soul. Most Christians are yet carnal, they do not understand anybody who insists on pressing through to Jesus. So long as one is just an ordinary Christian, nobody pays any attention. But let him start out to follow on to know the Lord and there will be lifted eyebrows and shrugged shoulders and caustic remarks. I imagine that some in this crowd were irritated at this woman: " Why can't she be satisfied to be among those present and stay back where she belongs? " So, even Christians will bid the desperate seeker to " let well enough alone," but the only way out is to push through the tumult singing,

" I'll go to Jesus, though my sin
Hath like a mountain rose:
I know His courts I'll enter in,
Whatever may oppose."

Whatever the need is, press through to Jesus! Some have been saved, but need another touch, not for salvation but for power. Some, like the blind man whom Jesus healed, have had one touch and see " men as trees walking " ; they live in a fog. They need another touch from the Lord. Whatever the need, pass through and you will find that " *as many as touched him were made whole* " (Mark 6: 56).

This woman also confessed publicly to her healing. She was just one of the crowd until she exercised faith, and then, in confession, she stood out from the crowd. Confession must accompany faith (Romans 10: 9, 10).

Our Lord would not let her steal the blessing. Many

blessings have been lost through failure to confess them. Whosoever believeth on Him should not be ashamed to confess Him. *"They looked unto him, and were lightened: and their faces were not ashamed"* (Psalm 34: 5).

Are you a sinner, a Naaman with the leprosy of sin? Earth's physicians cannot cure you. Press through to Jesus! Satan will block your way, he will let you join the church, reform, do ANYTHING BUT TOUCH JESUS. He will make any concession or compromise, so long as you do not touch the Lord and receive His virtue. But your case is desperate: stop nowhere short of His presence!

"Come, ye weary, heavy-laden, lost and ruined by the fall;
If you tarry till you're better, you will never come at all.
Let not conscience make you linger, nor of fitness fondly dream;
All the fitness He requireth is to feel your need of Him."

Mind you, this woman did not ask the Lord to touch her; SHE TOUCHED HIM. Some have been waiting for years for God to touch them in some mysterious experience or feeling. But Jesus of Nazareth is passing by, and you have only to press through and humbly touch Him. "Lord, I touch Thee; I take Thee, I trust Thee; I thank Thee,"—make that your experience! Press through to Jesus!

IX

"THE FOOLISHNESS OF GOD"

"*The foolishness of God is wiser than men.*"—I CORINTHIANS 1: 25.

IN Paul's day the Gospel of Jesus Christ was foolishness to the world. It is just as foolish today when lived and preached in its original simplicity by the power of the Holy Spirit. But most Christians today do not like the embarrassment of going to Christ without the camp, bearing His reproach: they do not want to be thought queer, and they must keep up with the Joneses. So, in order to escape being identified with the foolishness of God, we have toned down both the preaching and practice of the Gospel by trying to adapt it to the wisdom of this world.

There are those who foolishly imagine that the world is growing better and that, therefore, the Gospel will not meet the same reaction from this age that it met centuries ago. But human nature has not changed, and the present world system is still of the old Adam. "The natural man cannot receive the things of the Spirit of God"; "the carnal mind is enmity against God," and "they that are in the flesh cannot please God." The present world set-up is of the devil, just as it always has been, and when the pure and undiluted Gospel of Jesus Christ is preached in power, it is just as foolish to this age of radios and airplanes as it was when Paul wrote to the Corinthians.

There are not and cannot be any points of contact where the message of redemption can be fitted to the wisdom of this world. There are no points of similarity; there are only points of contrast. The Gospel is contrary to this world at every turn. It runs against the grain of this age from start to finish. It springs from a different source; it follows a different course; it arrives at a different conclusion. It denies everything that the world affirms, and everything which it affirms the world denies. If God be true, every natural man is a liar and there are no exceptions at any point. This world—and I do not mean merely our so-called lower order of vicious sinners, gangsters and hoodlums, but this educated, cultured, even religious, but unregenerate, world—has its own wisdom, its own interpretation of life, and its own standard of living. Over against that stands the supernatural revelation, the Gospel of Jesus Christ, and they are as far apart as east from west, and never the twain shall meet. All that this world calls wisdom God calls foolishness, and God's wisdom has always been and will be the laughing-stock of this world.

To begin with, the Gospel of Jesus Christ utterly contradicts the wisdom of this world as to the natural condition of man. This world talks education: God demands regeneration. This world says we need culture: God says we need Calvary. This world rates men by colour and bank account and by the social register and by ancestry: God sees only sinners and says, "*There is no difference: for all have sinned, and come short of the glory of God.*" Men judge by the number and nature of sins we commit and stage contests on: "Which is the greatest sin?" God sees sin, the nature back of the acts of sin, the soil from which the foul weeds grow. We grade sinners all the way from the vicious up to the respectable, but, with God, Nicodemus was just as lost as Barabbas, and the rich young ruler was as hopeless as the unrepentant thief on the cross. Sin is missing the mark and a miss is as bad as a mile. Whether one lives on the boulevard or in the backwoods, whether mayor or bootblack, "rich man, poor man, beggar-man, thief"—"*all have sinned,*" and "*there is no difference.*" Without Christ we may be rich sinners, educated sinners, moral sinners, religious sinners, baptized sinners, but still we are sinners.

Of course this world resents such a clear-cut classification of all men as saints or sinners, lost or saved. Someone argued recently that there are too many shades and grades of people to lump them arbitrarily into only two divisions. But that is exactly what God does: the Gospel knows only men out of Christ, and men in Christ; and the Lord Jesus stands in the midst of humanity dividing to the right and the left with that thrust of the two-edged Sword: "*He that is not with me is against me; and he that gathereth not with me scattereth abroad.*"

This world by its wisdom believes that the natural man can be cultivated and refined until he can pass inspection at the judgment bar of God. But the Gospel entertains no such hope for the fallen sons of Adam. In sin did our mothers conceive us. "*That which is born of the flesh is flesh,*" and it remains flesh which cannot please God. Whether it breathe the atmosphere of a dozen universities or the foul odours of a back alley; whether it drive a Pierce-Arrow or push an apple cart, flesh is flesh. The most decent and cultured, upstanding and outstanding character without a second birthday when he believed on Jesus Christ to the saving of the soul is as lost as the worst gangster in Sing Sing.

Of course, this sounds like foolishness to this world, and so it is—the *" foolishness of God."* And this foolishness of God is just as diametrically opposed to the wisdom of the world when it comes to the remedy for man's condition and the way to be saved. The wisdom of men believes that any religion is good and that Abana and Pharpar are as effective as Jordan for Naamans sick with the leprosy of sin. But the Gospel declares that there is one Mediator between God and men, the Man Christ Jesus; *" neither is there salvation in any other: for there is none other name under heaven given among men, whereby we must be saved."* The Gospel is God's Good News about a crucified Christ Who died for our sins and rose for our justification. The world laughs at such preaching of the Cross, ridicules " slaughter-house theology," and tramples under foot the blood of Christ without the shedding of which there is no remission of sins.

It is natural that a blood-bought redemption should not appeal to the wisdom of men, for there is nothing in it that suits our reason and pride. The very idea of being saved by One Who could not save Himself! Who ever heard of living through Someone Who died? It sounds ridiculous, this being blessed by One Who was Himself made a curse! Who can make sense of being justified by One Who was Himself condemned? So the world argues against this Gospel of " No Other Name " just as the antediluvians laughed at Noah's Ark, and the unbelievers doubted the Passover blood, and the skeptics reasoned about the efficacy of looking at the brazen serpent. John 3: 16 leaves no place for human pride or merit: for eternal life is the free gift of God which cannot be earned or learned, but only can be accepted or refused. Of course, that takes the wind out of the sails of human wisdom and naturally the wiseacres of earth have raged against it, but God's way stands: "*Believe on the Lord Jesus Christ and thou shalt be saved.*"

Beginning at conversion, the Christian walks by faith and not by sight; he lives by the faith of the Son of God. And once again the foolishness of God cuts across the wisdom of men. Man insists upon seeing before believing; he lives by his five senses, but here comes a different way of living by the sixth sense of faith.

Right here, we sadly confess that so few professing Christians really live by faith nowadays that the world is not stirred into reaction against it. For their name is legion who profess to trust Christ for salvation and commit their souls to Him for eternity, but who fall back upon the wisdom of men for their daily living. Forgetting that He Who offered up His Son for us all hath with Him also freely given us all things, they live by their own wits and wills from day to day, living not only in the flesh, but by the flesh.

But once in a while there emerges one who really takes this business seriously, who stakes everything upon what God has said and sets his face like a flint to "endure as seeing Him Who is invisible," knowing that he shall not be ashamed. And when we say "living by faith" we do not mean that Sunday-morning sort that sings, "My Faith Looks Up to Thee," and then lives looking backward and forward and inside and outside, but never upward. We mean a breath-taking, mountain-moving, soul-stirring, devil-defying faith that marches across all the principles, plans and purposes of the old Adam, alarms the devil and sets the angels rejoicing. We mean a faith that tramps across moods and feelings, laughs at the spectres and goblins of the mind, takes the Bible at what it says and shouts, "*Let God be true, but every man a liar!*" Such a life is no mere grading up from the natural, just an advance from a lower range of experience. It is a supernatural life, the life of Christ lived in us by the faith of the Son of God. No wonder an uncomprehending world calls it impractical mysticism; for it is another manifestation of "*the foolishness of God.*"

He who sets out to travel this road will find himself on no crowded highway; for this way leads to life and few there be that find it. He will find himself beset by all the powers of darkness. Satan will marshal his most subtle wiles against such a dare-saint and court him as an angel of light. Even the Church, which has so generally abandoned the walk of faith for the walk by sight, will offer scant encouragement. And at home his foes may be those of his own household. For nothing so alarms the devil as a Christian who actually insists upon taking the Gospel seriously and trusting God for such things as health and money, as well as for a home in heaven. The average Christian causes Satan scant uneasiness, but one of these faith-walkers can cause no end of trouble; for he demonstrates the very thing the devil hates most—"*the foolishness of God.*" So all the hosts of darkness conspire against God's Venturers, and often the way seems lonely. But there are other precious souls faring along it. Above all, there is Another Who trod that way Himself and Who lives in us to travel it now. It is a mighty adventure, but if you are determined to tread that trail, expect to be counted a "*fool for Christ's sake;*" for this is the outliving of "*the foolishness of God.*"

Just as the faith-life of the individual believer is a contradiction of the wisdom of this world, so is the collective life of believers in the Church. But, alas, just as Christians have abandoned the "*life by the faith of the Son of God*" and fallen back upon the arm of flesh, so have churches lost their peculiar identity and become like the clubs and societies of this world, aping the present age in membership, message, motive, and method.

From the beginning, God has hid His secrets from the wise and prudent and has revealed them unto babes. Not many mighty, wise, and noble after the flesh have been called, but God has chosen the foolish things, the weak, base, and despised, and things which are not, that no flesh should glory in His presence. He has chosen the poor of this world, rich in faith and heirs of the Kingdom. In the Old Testament, He chose Israel and selected a despised race, one that gets scant notice in secular history, for the instrument of His purpose. Then came His only begotten Son, born in a stable, ministering to lowly people, dying a criminal's death, despised and rejected of men. And His Church He formed from humble and poor disciples without genius, wealth, or honour, the hated sect of Nazarenes. So long as the Church ran true to form, God prospered it. But when Constantine made it fashionable and respectable and joined with the world for prestige and honour, the decline began. Today the Church courts the world and pays tribute to the pride and wisdom of man; it has lost its original identity. The peculiar people have become a popular people at home in this world.

We cannot get over the ridiculous delusion that, the more wealth and learning and ability we add to our church membership, the stronger we are. We catch ourselves saying, " If that man were in the church what a power he could be! " We fish for more " influential " members and think we have advantaged the Lord by adding a banker to the church roll or an artist to the choir. When will we learn that all this is repulsive to God? Human cleverness, brilliance, wealth, and wit cannot please Him. If we are gifted we are none the better; if we are not gifted we are none the worse. God is not hampered by our lack of ability, nor is He advantaged by our abundance of it. It is all of grace lest any man should boast, and it is nothing with God to help, whether with few or many.

Of course, all this is foolishness to the world for it knows no resource but the wit and will of man. And even the professing Church has been led astray to value in its membership the gifts of man above the gifts of the Spirit. But "*the foolishness of God*" is still wiser than men, and His weakness stronger than men, if by simple faith we dare to prove them.

Again, the message of the Church cuts across the wisdom of men. It is the preaching of Christ and Him crucified, and that is always a stumbling-block and foolishness to the world. The world by its wisdom knew not God, and God is pleased by the foolishness of preaching to save them that believe. And to these who believe, "*the foolishness of God*" is found to be the wisdom of God and His weakness is found to be power (I Corinthians 1: 24).

Not only does the message itself contradict all human wisdom, but the very manner of its delivery does the same. For the Gospel is not to be preached in words of men's wisdom, but in demonstration of the Spirit and of power, that our faith should not stand in the wisdom of men, but in the power of God. For God's revelation is not spoken in the words which man's wisdom teaches, but in the wisdom which the Holy Ghost teaches, comparing spiritual things with spiritual. Many a young Apollos has set out to preach with the tongues of men and of angels, only to learn from some obscure Priscilla and Aquila that he is but sounding brass and clanging cymbal! Here is no parade ground for human eloquence: for the Gospel that cuts across man's wisdom at every other point makes no compromise even in the manner of its delivery.

The message of the Church is delivered also with a motive power utterly different—the power of the Holy Spirit. Human enthusiasm and fervour, however earnest and well-intentioned, are but the stimulants of the natural man, "*wine wherein is excess*"; but we must be filled with the Spirit. Nadab and Abihu offer strange fire today in many a sanctuary, and "pep" is substituted for Pentecostal power. To be sure, this is foolishness to a world that runs only on its own steam, but now and then God raises up a man like Moody to show that He can work wonders with a most unlikely instrument, since it is not by might nor power, but by His Spirit. Today, alas, the Church has slipped at this point, and in many a pulpit Jannes and Jambres try to perform, by tricks of personal magnetism, the wonders of God. Human enthusiasm and fervour can, indeed, do many remarkable things, but only by the power of God can we preach and practice the Gospel.

Along with this, the Gospel works by a different method from the wisdom of men. God's methods with His Church have seemed utterly ridiculous from the very beginning. Our Lord called twelve obscure men, fishermen and common folk, and one of them a traitor. The early Church went out simply to witness to Jesus Christ, with no elaborate organization or program. Never did an undertaking appear more hopeless to a world that plans and schemes and worships the god of efficiency. But that early fellowship upset the world. Today the Church dares not risk the "*foolishness*" and weakness of God, and so patterns after the world: its organization, methods, financial programs, campaigns, drives, educational systems have been borrowed from the present age; its whole life has been modeled after the business, educational, financial, and social set-up of modern man. David is hauling the ark on a new cart. The spirit of this commercialized age has invaded the sanctuary. Ministers' studies have become offices. Corporation methods have become more important than consecrated men. Men work in church with the spirit of the counting-house. Human busyness has obscured the Father's Business. The best church, nowadays, is the one with the most impressive statistics. The wisdom of man has become adviser to the Church of Christ, and everywhere today the results are painfully evident. Submerged in debt, shorn of power, and crowded with unregenerated members, the churches vainly try still newer methods and seek by high-pressure rallies and cheer-leader enthusiasm to do God's work in man's way. Not until we repent of our folly and sin, and dare to prove the foolishness and weakness of God in simple Spirit-filled living and testimony, shall we recover our Pentecost.

Finally, " *the foolishness of God* " utterly contradicts the wisdom of men when it looks toward the future. Men count heavily on evolution and dream high dreams of the parliament of man and the federation of the world. But the Gospel declares that our boasted progress shall head into ruin, and civilization crash into catastrophe, and that Jesus shall come back personally just as He went away, to reign in victory. Of course, such an idea seems only the wildest sort of fanaticism to the world, and perhaps no other doctrine of the faith has met more ridicule. It is especially unpopular today because it crashes headlong into all our modern philosophy of progress built on the hypotheses of evolution. Even the Church, save for a faithful few who still read the signs in the light of the Word, has lost its vision of a personal return of the Lord and has substituted for it the Christianizing of the world. Naturally, with both the world at large and most of the professing Church itself set against it, the Scriptural message of the Lord's return has felt the full measure of the scorn of men. Scoffers in abundance arise saying, "Where is the promise of His coming?" and many are blind to the portents of His near appearing.

So, from start to finish, at every point the Gospel of Jesus Christ still contradicts the wisdom of men. That is why most Christians still belong to the poor and plain walks of life—not because God puts a premium on poverty and plainness, nor because unlearned and lowly people are favourites with Him, but because man finds it so hard to renounce his own wealth and will and wisdom. One must turn and become as a little child to travel God's way and nobody wants to be childlike, it does not sound smart nor sophisticated. All this business of believing without seeing and being dead to self and being made strong through weakness and wise by becoming fools—it sounds like foolishness to moderns who are so afraid of being gullible and stupid that they are perhaps the most stupid of all generations.

But "*the foolishness of God*" is such only to those who perish. Believe it, receive it, live by it and it becomes wisdom this world can never know, that divine wisdom which belongs to those who know the secret of the Lord, who by willing to do His will know of the doctrine. The weakness of God is such only to those who will not receive it. To those who are saved it is the power of God, the power to do all things through Christ Who strengthens us. God has promised to destroy the wisdom of the wise and to bring to nothing the understanding of the prudent. " *Let no man deceive himself. If any man among you seemeth to be wise, let him become a fool that he may be wise.*"

Blessed are the fools for Christ's sake who dare to demonstrate to this unbelieving world the " *foolishness and weakness of God* " *!*

X

LEARNING, LIVING, LOOKING

NOW and then in the New Testament one finds the great outstanding doctrines of our faith compassed within a very few verses. Such a passage is Titus 2: 11–14. One might think of verses 11 and 14 as a frame for verses 12 and 13. In this mighty framework notice what tremendous truths are set forth.

"*The grace of God,*" "*salvation,*" "*hath appeared to all men*"—there is the incarnation; "*who gave himself for us*" —there is the atonement; "*that he might redeem us*"— there is redemption; "*and purify unto himself*"—there is sanctification; "*a peculiar people*"—there you have separation; "*zealous of good works*"—there you have works. There are few other passages where two verses tell so much.

Within this wonderful frame we find in verses 12 and 13 the Christian experience set forth. It is as though what our Lord has done for us is presented in verses 11 and 14, and then that what we are to do by and for our Lord is shown in the verses between. Notice also that the two advents are given, the first appearing to all men in verse 11, and the second, "*the glorious appearing of the great God and our Saviour Jesus Christ,*" in verse 13. Between this advent of grace and the advent of glory our duty is set forth, the practical side of our experience within the framework of these eternal truths.

You will observe that our experience is threefold: It is an experience of learning, of living, and of looking.

It is first an experience of learning. "*Teaching us*" implies that we must learn. Perhaps "*disciplining us*" would be a better translation. The Christian life begins with a B. A. degree—Born Again—but, still, we must learn. Our Lord promised to give rest to those who came to Him (Matthew 11: 28). But in the very next verse He says: "*Take my yoke upon you, and learn of me; for I am meek and lowly in heart: and ye shall find rest unto your souls.*" There is a sense in which His rest is an obtainment and another sense in which it is an attainment. We receive His rest when we receive Him; but only as we learn of Him and practice His presence do we realize His rest. One finds a kindred thought in Hebrews 4: 10, 11: "*For he that is entered into his rest, he also hath ceased from his own works, as God did from his. Let us labour therefore to enter into that rest.*"

Grace does not involve anything we may *earn*, but it involves much that we may *learn*. "*The Comforter, which is the Holy Ghost, whom the Father will send in my name, he shall teach you all things, and bring all things to your remembrance, whatsoever I have said unto you*" (John 14: 26). Luke tells us that his Gospel was a record only of what Jesus began to do and teach (Acts 1: 1). Paul says: "*We speak, not in the words which man's wisdom teacheth, but which the Holy Ghost teacheth*" (I Corinthians 2: 13).

We must be disciples if we are to be doers. Through the Word, through prayer, through meditation, through worship and books and conversation and godly teachers and daily experiences, God teaches us by the Spirit, and blessed is he that heareth. Let us give heed to the "*things . . . written for our learning*" (Romans 15: 4). Let us not be among those "*ever learning, and never able to come to the knowledge of the truth.*" We are to continue in the things we have learned (II Timothy 3: 14). We are to learn to maintain good works (Titus 3: 14) and, like Paul, to learn in whatsoever state we are, therewith to be content (Philippians 4: 11).

But there is a definite purpose in the words of our passage: "*Teaching us that . . .*" We are taught in order that we may do something. Our Lord told His disciples that they were to go forth, "*teaching them to observe all things whatsoever I have commanded you.*" It is not enough to teach nor to learn the things commanded. We have not really learned them until we have learned to observe them.

Thus learning must be translated into living. "*Teaching us that, denying ungodliness and worldly lusts, we should live soberly, righteously, and godly, in this present world.*" You will observe that the negative side is given first: "*denying ungodliness and worldly lusts.*" There is something to shun in the Christian life, in spite of all this modern insistence that we should not preach on the "don'ts." It is true that salvation is spelled neither "do" nor "don't," but "done"; yet, in the experience of living, there is something to deny as well as to do. The Lord Jesus Christ said: "*If any man will come after me, let him deny himself, and take up his cross, and follow me.*" He bade us cut off that which offends (Mark 9: 42–50). We are to lay aside every weight and besetting sin. "*Be not drunk with wine, wherein is excess.*"

The Word demands separation, and all Scripture is profitable for reproof and correction, as well as for doctrine and instruction in righteousness. Thus the negative side is recognized equally with the positive. Paul admonished Timothy to "*reprove, rebuke,*" as well as exhort. Achan's wedge and wardrobe often hinder the victory, and we must destroy the accursed thing from among us (Joshua 7: 12).

Thus, in this passage we are instructed to deny ungodliness and the lusts of this age. Some of these lusts are very fashionable and socially respectable nowadays, but if they are of this age we must drop them. "*Love not the world, neither the things that are in the world. If any man love the world, the love of the Father is not in him. For all that is in the world, the lust of the flesh, and the lust of the eyes, and the pride of life, is not of the Father, but is of the world. And the world passeth away, and the lust thereof: but he that doeth the will of God abideth forever.*"

Then the positive side of this experience is stated in a threefold ascending order. We are to live soberly, righteously, and godly—soberly, with regard to self; righteously, with regard to others; godly, with regard to God. Thus the order progresses.

We are to live soberly, not drunk with earth's wines—any of its false intoxications, enthusiasms, stimulations. We limit the admonition of Ephesians 5: 18 to physical wine, but there are mental and even religious stimulants by which flesh seeks to glory in His presence—even at church.

We are to live righteously, not with self-righteousness, law-righteousness, "*not having mine own righteousness, which is of the law, but that which is through the faith of Christ, the righteousness which is of God by faith*" (Philippians 3: 9). Our only righteousness is Christ Himself, made unto us righteousness (I Corinthians 1: 30), and our living righteously is simply the outliving of the inliving Christ.

We are to live godly. Again, godliness is simply the nature of God, implanted at regeneration, outworking in daily conduct, and manifested in the divine character of the in-dwelling Christ. Do we realize that our new nature is nothing less than the very nature of God within us, that our eternal life is the very supernatural life of God Himself? Godliness is God-likeness, and God-like living is of course God within us by His Holy Spirit, living His own life through our surrendered wills.

This sober, righteous, and godly life is to be lived "*in this present world.*" We are not to hide in a cave like medieval mystics. This life is to be worked out right here in this commonplace and unromantic workaday world. God's purpose with us was never to develop a race of ascetics with hands folded on breasts, gazing heavenward, singing evermore about the sweet by-and-by. His purpose is to develop Christlike characters who can stand the wear and tear of the here-and-now. Beware of that tendency to find in devotional books and the mysticism of the recluse an emotional escape from reality by which you dodge the daily grind. The Lord Jesus Christ spent His life in rough and rocky Palestine, with ordinary people amid the matter-of-fact problems of the day-by-day. We must follow Christ. This present world may not seem a very ideal place, but it is an ideal place for God's present purpose with believers. Heaven is the ideal place for its particular purpose, but we are now on earth, and it is an ideal training ground, with all its hardships and handicaps, its weal and woe. Do not try to escape by withdrawing into yourself or hiding in some retreat far removed from earth's sin and shame. This life is to be lived amid the currents of today, "where cross the crowded ways of life."

Finally, this life is an experience of looking. "*Looking*

for that blessed hope, and the glorious appearing of the great God and our Saviour Jesus Christ." We not only look back to a finished redemption in His first appearing when "*the grace of God that bringeth salvation*" appeared. We look unto Him Who shall appear the second time, apart from sin unto salvation (Hebrews 9: 28, R.V.). He came first to redeem us; now He comes to receive us! So we live, "*looking for and hasting unto the coming of the day of God*" (II Peter 3: 12), "*for our conversation* ("*citizenship,*" *R.V.*) *is in heaven; from whence also we look for the Saviour, the Lord Jesus Christ*" (Philippians 3: 20).

One of the favourite attitudes of those who show scant interest in our Lord's return is that the main thing is to be ready, and that if we are ready, we need not bother about whether His coming be near or far. It certainly is important to be ready, and the Scriptures emphasize that truth throughout. But these New Testment Christians were not only ready; they were eager, expectant, thrilled with anticipation, and earnestly looking for their Lord's return. No amount of clever exegesis can obscure that fact. They were not satisfied merely to be ready. It is one thing to be ready for an expected visitor, but quite another to look eagerly for him. I have been prepared more than once for a caller when I was not thrilled with anticipation, and I am quite sure that in my rounds of visitation there were those who were ready for my call who were not joyfully expectant!

If you grew up with a sister, you will recall that you could tell when a regular friend was going to call on her and when she was expecting her true lover. She was ready for the ordinary friend, but there was no exhilaration about it. But when he whom she loved was to appear—ah, there were eagerness, anticipation, and how slowly moved the hours!

One wonders about these believers who say they are ready for their souls' Lover, but who act as though it did not matter whether He ever appeared or not. The New Testament hope carried more than readiness; it carried hilarious anticipation. And one feels that joyful expectancy is a proof of readiness!

Truly blessed is our threefold experience. There is Someone from Whom to learn, Someone by Whom and for Whom to live, Someone for Whom to look. Between His advents of grace and glory, let us learn, let us live, let us look.

XI

THE HEAVENLY VISION

"*I was not disobedient unto the heavenly vision.*"—ACTS 26: 19.

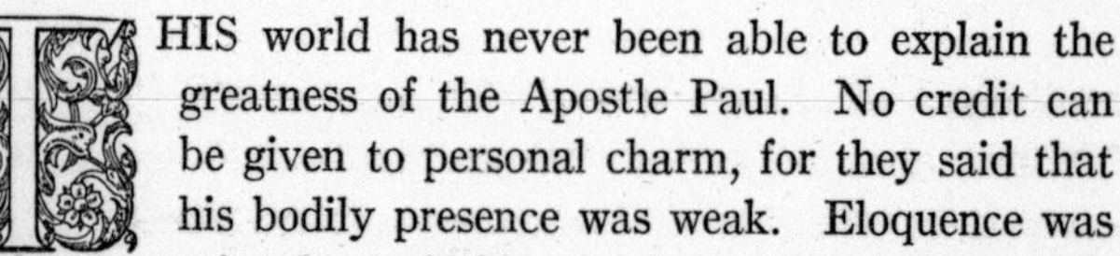

HIS world has never been able to explain the greatness of the Apostle Paul. No credit can be given to personal charm, for they said that his bodily presence was weak. Eloquence was not the secret, for they said his speech was contemptible. It was not learning, for, although he was an educated man, he counted it but loss and abhorred every display of human wisdom. It was not popularity and "pull," for he was an outcast, a despised Jew, a vagabond in an unfriendly world. It was not influence, for he did not have enough of that to keep out of jail.

If Paul were measured according to the standard used by many churches in calling a pastor, he would fail on all counts! Yet he shook a world and his name is stamped indelibly as the greatest of Gospel preachers, and all because one day on the Damascus road he turned a corner and met Jesus Christ. From that day he lived, with reckless abandon, an en-Christed life, a torch set on fire from heaven, a human instrument for God's own personal use, a man whom no amount of pain or persecution could turn from the terrific intensity of "*This one thing I do.*"

Such men are irresistible. You cannot stop them. Put

them in jail, and they pray down earthquakes. Hamper them with thorns in the flesh, and they glory in their infirmities. Sentence them to death, and they shout, "*To die is gain! To depart and be with Christ is far better.*" You cannot head them off, even when you take off their heads!

Paul's biography is summed up in his word to Agrippa: "*I was not disobedient unto the heavenly vision.*" The story of his life might be set forth in three phases: A heavenly vision; a holy venture; a happy victory. You will observe that when Paul met the Lord, he asked Him two questions: "*Who art thou, Lord?*" and "*Lord, what wilt thou have me to do?*" (Acts 9: 5, 6). Here we have a "Who" question and a "What" question. The vision is covered by the "Who" question and the venture by the "What" question.

First, then, is the heavenly vision: Paul saw the Lord. There can be no Christian man, message or ministry without a vision of the Lord. We need to see the Lord as did Isaiah, and cry, "*Woe is me!*"; like Habakkuk when his body trembled and rottenness entered his bones; like Job when he abhorred himself; like Daniel when his comeliness turned to corruption; like John when he fell at His feet as one dead. Men have seen books and schools and teachers, but they have not seen the Lord. Moody used to say that when Moses was in Egypt to deliver Israel the first time, he "looked this way and that way" and he got into trouble; but the second time he looked only one way and he saw the Lord; "*he endured as seeing him who is invisible.*" Men have not beheld the Lamb of God; they are not looking unto Jesus; they have not looked and been lightened so that their faces are not ashamed. Consequently, too many like Ahimaaz of old run to carry tidings, but have seen only a tumult. Modern Elijahs, not having met the Lord at Cherith, are unable to pray down fire at Carmel.

We must first face the " Who " question before we are ready for the " What " question. There is no use in asking, " What wilt thou have me to do? " before we have asked " Who art thou, Lord? " Some of us are afraid to ask " What? " because we have never gotten established on the " Who? " If we had more faith in Him, we should have less fear of what He wants us to do. We should not fear His command to go into all the world if we realized that HE is with us.

The WHO must precede the WHAT. *" Thine eyes shall see the king in his beauty; they shall behold the land that is very far off "* (Isaiah 33: 17). The vision of the Fair King must come before the vision of the Far Country. Isaiah saw the Lord and the vision brought conviction: *" Woe is me."* It brought confession of individual guilt: *" I am a man of unclean lips; "* of collective guilt: *" I dwell in the midst of a people of unclean lips."* We do not realize how unclean we are, as persons or as a people, until we have seen the Lord. Somewhere I have read of a washerwoman who was very proud of the whiteness of her day's wash, until there came a snowfall and she saw her work against the background of the spotless snow. So we do not realize how foul is our best until we see it against the holiness of the Lord.

Then, Isaiah's vision brought cleansing. The angel touched his lips with a coal from the altar and said, *" Thine iniquity is taken away and thy sin purged."* Too many are whitewashed, but not washed white. If ever we are to be cleansed and made holy, we must see the Lord. We live in a shallow generation that has never come to grips with eternal issues and knows nothing of conviction, repentance, regeneration and sanctification, because it has never met God. Ministers are trained for the pulpit as others are for medicine or law, and go out to preach salvation without ever having met the Saviour. Many have conferred only with flesh and blood and need a trip to Arabia instead of a vacation. More than one aspiring and perspiring Apollos needs to meet Priscilla and Aquila and learn the way of the Lord more perfectly.

Churches are filled with unregenerate members who have signed cards and filed down aisles and joined the church without ever having been conscious of sin or humbled in repentance enough to cry, "*Woe is me . . . for mine eyes have seen the king.*" Men dare to make the holy venture without having seen the heavenly vision. Sunday-school teachers are chosen for the gift of gab. Business men are appointed to be deacons waiting on the tables of the church without ever having waited on God. Christian work is undertaken by Jacobs who have never been changed to Israels, have never met God face to face, and have no power with God or men. "*Where there is no vision, the people perish.*" Men have seen the Church, they have seen doctrine, but they have not seen God.

After the heavenly vision, Paul made the holy venture. After the "Who" question came the "What" question: "*What wilt thou have me to do?*" He not only saw the Lord: he went to work for the Lord. We read in Acts 16: 10: "*After he had seen the vision, immediately we endeavoured to go.*" That is always God's order, the vision and then the venture. We have said that Isaiah's vision brought conviction, confession and cleansing. It brought more. It brought a call: "*Whom shall I send and who will go for us?"* It brought consent: *"Here am I; send me."* It brought a commission: *"And he said, Go."* After seeing comes service. After the "Lo" comes the "Go." And, thank God, after the "Go" comes the "Lo": *"Go ye therefore . . . and, lo, I am with you . . ."*

Judson saw the Lord—and he saw Burma. Livingstone saw the Lord—and he saw Africa. Paton saw the Lord—and he saw lost cannibals. Moody saw the Lord—and he saw a lost world. God does not want mere adoration, He wants action. Too often we sing, "Take my life and let it be," and we really mean for God to LET IT BE, to lay it up on a shelf and do nothing with it! Someone has said that vision without work is visionary; work without vision is mercenary; vision and work are missionary.

So Paul followed the "Who" with the "What" and for all the rest of his life he was not disobedient unto the heavenly vision. We claim to have seen the Lord today, but many of us have never faced His will for our lives. God has a purpose for every one of us, somewhere that He wants us to be, something He wants us to do, and we never can please God anywhere else. We may do lovely things, be successful, but we shall always be haunted with a sense of having missed God's best. Woodrow Wilson once spoke of being "defeated by our secondary successes." Many a man has missed God's success for him, satisfied with his own. It is said that Sir Thomas Lipton, the famous sportsman, while showing his trophies and prizes to a friend, cried with a sweep of the hand, "And I'd give them all for the one I didn't get [The American cup]"! How sad to come to life's close having amassed all the prizes and trophies of earth and then to miss the prize of the high calling of God in Christ Jesus! What better epitaph could any wish than

God's Word about David, that he served his generation by the will of God? Blessed is he who can come to death saying in his little sphere what our Lord could say in His great sphere: "*I have glorified thee on the earth: I have finished the work which thou gavest me to do.*"

Are you where God wants you, "*perfect and complete in all the will of God*"? God told Elijah to go to Cherith and hide by the brook and added, "*I have commanded the ravens to feed thee THERE.*" Later God told Elijah to go to Zarephath and "*dwell THERE,*" and added, "*I have commanded a widow woman THERE to sustain thee.*" Mind you, He did not promise to feed Elijah just anywhere. He did not say, "Just ramble over the country anywhere you like and I will feed you." It was limited to THERE, the place of God's will. God provides only where He guides. The place of His purpose is the place of His power and His provision. But we must be THERE.

So, the heavenly vision must be followed by the holy venture. With Isaiah there were the vision and voice, the volunteer. With Paul the "What" followed the "Who."

Finally, Paul realized happy victory. "*I have fought a good fight, I have finished my course, I have kept the faith: Henceforth there is laid up for me a crown of righteousness, which the Lord, the righteous judge, shall give me at that day: and not to me only but unto all them also that love his appearing.*" Paul may have seemed a victim, but he was a victor. Appearing before Nero, he may have looked like a failure, standing there alone amidst the glory of Roman imperialism. But it has been said that "it is not without significance that today we call our dogs 'Nero' and our boys 'Paul'!"

He called himself "*the prisoner of Jesus Christ.*" He may

have seemed to be the prisoner of men, of Rome, but he knew that back of earthly incarceration stood He Who holds not only the keys of hell and death but of every circumstance of earth. And, although he came to life's close calling only for an overcoat and a few books, his was the incorruptible crown, the reward men, blinded by the tinsel trophies of earth, cannot see. What matters it, when we come in from life's adventure, whether we bear in our hands any visible tokens of victory, any rewards of earth, if we can say, "*I saw the Lord,*" and, "*I was not disobedient unto the heavenly vision*"?

XII

"IF ANY MAN THIRST"

"Now on the last day, the great day of the feast, Jesus stood and cried, saying, If any man thirst, let him come unto me, and drink.

"He that believeth on me, as the scripture hath said, from within him shall flow rivers of living water.

"But this spake he of the Spirit, which they that believed on him were to receive: for the Spirit was not yet given; because Jesus was not yet glorified."—JOHN 7: 37–39, R.V.

OUR Lord was at the feast of tabernacles. It is very likely that He had just been observing a peculiar ceremony which was a custom at that time. It seems that each day a priest with a golden pitcher went to the pool of Siloam followed by a throng of people. Filling the pitcher at the pool, he bore it down the streets amid the shouting and singing of the multitude and the sound of trumpets and cymbals. When he reached the temple he poured out the water by the altar while all the people sang, "*Therefore with joy shall ye draw water out of the wells of salvation*" (Isaiah 12: 3). It was such a hilarious occasion that, according to Lightfoot, it was said, "Whoever has not witnessed it has never seen rejoicing at all."

Doubtless our Lord had just witnessed this ceremony and, although it was very impressive, He must have been struck with the futility of it all. For, although these jubilant multitudes sang and shouted and went into raptures, after it all was over they went home with their same old heartaches and cares and fears. Then, too, it was a perfect picture of the fact that the law, represented by the priest, and legalism and religiousness and ceremony, represented by the pouring out of the water, could never assuage the thirst of the human heart. And more than that, it symbolized the utter inability of the waters of earth, its pleasures and possessions and philosophies, to satisfy the weary soul. Men might make great ado over these things, might for the moment rejoice in them, but always they must go away thirsty, because they have forsaken the fountain of living waters and hewn them out cisterns, broken cisterns, that can hold no water (Jeremiah 2: 13).

But there stood among the throngs on this feast day One Who could satisfy the thirsty soul. While the worshippers sang, "*With joy shall ye draw water out of the wells of salvation,*" little did they realize that the fulfilment of that prophecy stood among them! And now, with the vivid contrast of the water-pouring ceremony before Him, the Lord Jesus did a most unusual thing, He stood and cried aloud to the throngs around Him. "*He stood and cried,*" —very rarely is that phrase used of our Lord. "*He shall not strive, nor cry; neither shall any man hear his voice in the streets*" (Matthew 12: 19), but here He went out of the ordinary, did the exceptional thing of standing, probably in some elevated position, and crying aloud to the multitude. Why did He do it? Because He had something exceptional and extraordinary to say! His soul had been moved within Him by the vain ceremony of the feast day and now He sets Himself against the hollow observance of the empty pitcher and cries, "*If any man thirst, let him come unto me and drink! He that believeth on me, as the scripture hath said, from within him shall flow rivers of living water!*"

It is as though He cried: "Ah, you thirst for something, you know not what. These hollow ceremonies, these ecstasies of the flesh, these empty pitchers from Siloam, these waters of earth can never satisfy. Come unto me and drink and I will give you living waters which shall become in you fountains of water springing up into everlasting life (John 4: 14), and rivers of water forever overflowing. '*Ho, every one that thirsteth, come ye to the waters*' (Isaiah 55: 1). '*Whosoever will, let him take the water of life freely*'" (Revelation 22: 17).

Nineteen centuries have gone their way, and today a thirsting world still hews its broken cisterns and seeks in poured-out waters of Siloam living waters that fail not. Ponce de Leon still looks for the fountain of youth. Modern fads and isms, psychologic tricks and philosophic cure-alls—these are golden pitchers from Siloam which are soon poured out. And what shall we say of thousands who go through all the motions of religion, even grow ecstatic like these Jews at the feast, yet go away unsatisfied as ever? Amidst it all stands One Who is the Bread of Life, Who invites the labouring and the laden to come unto Him and rest (John 6: 35; Matthew 11: 28). Whosoever lives and believes in Him shall never die (John 11: 26). In Him, though the outward man perish, yet the inward man is renewed day by day (II Corinthians 4: 16). He is the soul's fountain of youth. If any man thirst, let him come unto Him and drink and he shall have within himself a fountain of living waters overflowing in torrents of blessing.

That, of course, is the first application of this precious passage—Christ's invitation to a lost world. But I am thinking now of another situation painfully evident today: thousands of Christians, believers, saved people, whose actual, daily experience is more like the emptied pitcher from Siloam than it is like the living fountain with its rivers of water. As I go about over the land, I am continually meeting preachers grieved over a defective experience, who are convinced that they have missed something and that surely there must be more in the filling of the Spirit than they have ever understood. They are good men, able men, devout men, but many of them seem to have stopped short of that utter abandon in which men lose themselves to become blazing firebrands for God, flaming torches by which He sets on fire a smug and sanctimonious church and awakens to burning conviction a sleeping world. Some are willing to miss a blessing rather than give up a prejudice, but others are worried and deeply conscious that their fire is not Pentecostal fire but painted fire which does not burn!

I am continually meeting Christians whose experience is like getting all of a story except the point. Like the Jews at the feast, they have a happy day once in a while when they "scale the utmost height and catch a gleam of glory bright," but these are few and far between and soon "a sense of things real comes doubly strong." After one of his sermons, Andrew Murray asked a very pious woman, "How are you going on?" Her answer was, "Oh, just the way it always is, sometimes light and sometimes dark." "My dear sister," he asked, "where is that in the Bible?" She said, "We have day and night in nature, and just so it is in our souls." "No, no," he replied, "in the Bible we read, '*Thy sun shall no more go down.*'" But most believers today live in an eclipse.

Naturally, all this shows up in the fellowship of believers. Our churches go forth often, like Samson, to shake themselves, as at other times before, and know not that the power of the Lord in fulness of blessing has departed. There is no listening for the sound of a going in the mulberry trees. Having begun in the Spirit, they would perfect themselves in the flesh. Instead of more power, more wheels are added to the machine. There is no ministering to the Lord and fasting, so the Spirit has nothing to say. There being no devotion, there is no Dynamic and no direction. There is nothing about the average Christian or church to remind one of rivers of living water issuing from a well of water springing up into everlasting life. Indeed, one is reminded more of the occasional pouring out of water from the golden pitcher filled at Siloam.

It is plainly stated here that our Lord spoke of the Holy Spirit, so the whole difficulty today lies in a failure rightly to appreciate and appropriate the fulness of the Spirit. It is interesting to note that many of these thirsty Christians today have been much taught if not well taught; they have studied the Word carefully, have prayed earnestly, have sought deeper blessing, have gone from Bible conference to Bible conference, returning home in the fall laden with notebooks crammed with epigrams from teachers galore. I fear that altogether too many have "eagerly frequented doctor and saint, and heard great argument about it and about, but evermore have come out the same door wherein they went." Some have "surrendered" dozens of times; have followed Andrew Murray's "steps" for the blessing; have "claimed the blessing," and then tried to believe they had it, meanwhile driving off the fowls from the offering, like Abraham, until God should send the witness of the burning lamp. They have tried not to confuse the filling with the feeling, but after months or years they still do not wear the garments of praise instead of the spirit of heaviness, and many break down in defeatism or else move into extremist circles. (And right here remember the words of a mighty man of God of the last generation: "It were almost better for one to overstate the possibilities of sanctification in his eager grasp after holiness, than to understate them in his complacent satisfaction with a traditional unholiness. Certainly it is not an edifying spectacle to see a Christian worlding throwing stones at a Christian perfectionist.")

Now, it is evident that if our Lord meant for us to be living fountains sending forth torrents of living water then we have no business standing along Jordan's stormy banks casting wishful eyes toward Canaan's fair and happy land, where our possessions lie. We ought to be dwelling over there in that blessed experience which the saints have called, "the rest of faith," "perfect love," "the Spirit-filled life," "the victorious life," or "Christian perfection." On this feast day the Lord invited us to the fulness of the Spirit as well as to salvation, and it behooves us rightly to appreciate and appropriate what is here set forth.

We recognize, of course, that when we come to the Lord Jesus Christ at conversion and receive Him, the Holy Spirit indwells our hearts from regeneration. We know also that the Holy Spirit was given at Pentecost once for all. But here we believe with A. J. Gordon, that "it does not follow that every believer has by faith received that baptism. God's gift is one thing; our appropriation of that gift is quite another thing. As Christ, the second Person of the Godhead, came to earth to make atonement for sin and to give eternal life, and as sinners we must receive Him by faith in order to forgiveness and sonship, so the Holy Spirit, the third Person of the Godhead, came to earth to communicate the 'power from on high'; and we must as believers in like manner receive Him by faith in order to be qualified for service. Both gifts have been bestowed, but it is not what we have but what we know we have by a conscious, appropriating faith which determines our spiritual wealth."

The baptism of the Spirit is ours positionally, but, alas, what is ours positionally is not always our actual condition. It is one thing to have the blessing as our right and privilege, but quite another to be blessed experimentally. The average Christian is so ignorant of, or indifferent to, the filling of the Spirit that when he does realize and receive fulness of power, it truly is a second blessing to him, second only to regeneration. Said McConkey: "There is a fulness of the Holy Ghost which does not come to most Christians at conversion and, therefore, is, in point of time, a second blessing." And Dr. James M. Gray makes it clear: "I believe that the second work of grace . . . is a later crisis in the history of the believer, when he comes to realize the need of a holier life and a deeper experience of Christ. He then surrenders himself as a Christian to Christ more fully than he has yet done and comes into the Spirit to which he has been a stranger theretofore. It is the privilege of every believer to have this experience at the moment of his acceptance of Christ as Saviour and some do enter into its enjoyment then. Many do not, however, and when it comes to them, if it does, they regard it as a second work of grace and a baptism of the Holy Spirit."

In our zeal to escape false doctrines of a "second blessing" most Christians, we fear, have gone too far and denied any need of crisis or deeper experience in the life of the believer, except a gradual growth in grace. Now, for believers who recognized and appropriated the filling of the Spirit at conversion and who are being filled continually that is sufficient. But very few have done that, and, besides, it has been asked with real insight: "If we conceive of the Christian life as only a gradual growth in grace, is there not a danger that we come to regard this growth as both invisible and inevitable and so take little responsibility for its accomplishment?"

Many arguments have been employed against this experience, even by established Christians. The subjective aspect of just yielding and receiving has taken the place of the old emphasis our fathers placed on being overwhelmed with power coming down. The mighty old-fashioned down-crashing floods of power that inundated and submerged waiting saints have been ignored in favour of a rather tame and pale "receiving" that fails somehow to receive. Some say we are not to pray for power. If that is true, then the mighty men of God through the ages have been mistaken. Others contend that we do violence to the personality of the Holy Spirit in speaking of being filled as though He were like electricity. We can say only that "*filled*" is the New Testament word.

And what shall we say of the testimony of history? Think of George Fox, lying for days in a trance, and coming through to a new experience; Wesley and Whitefield praying until three in the morning, when the Spirit fell in great power; Christmas Evans convicted of a cold heart while on his way to preach and led to pray until his heart thawed out like the breaking up of a hard winter, and going on to preach with power, so that a gracious revival began and swept the country roundabout. Think of Burns of Kilsyth saying to his mother after a night of prayer, "God has given me Kilsyth today," and going forth to reap souls not only in Kilsyth but in all Scotland and in Inland China. And what shall we say of Finney who saw the Lord and then, set burning with the heavenly flame, moved out into a ministry of evangelism so marvelous that I am astounded that few Christians today seem to know anything of this giant of the Gospel. One thinks of the Moravians at Herrnhut, of A. J. Gordon in his midnight prayer meeting with George Needham, of Moody receiving such a blessing that he had to ask God to stay His hand, and testifying of it later: "I would not be back where I was before that blessed experience if you should give me all the world—it would be as the small dust of the balance." Say what you will, these men knew a day of crisis and, although salvation dated from an earlier day, mighty power for service dated from this day. When one reads the story of these powerful fountains of living water, he is more than ever impressed with the thought that most of us today are strangely like pitchers from Siloam! It ill becomes us dwarfs to differ with such giants of yesterday.

Well does F. B. Meyer ask us: "Are we experimentally possessed of the Pentecostal enduement? Are we willing to pay the price of it?" Pentecost is on the church calendar but it is not the churches' condition. Moody declared in Boston: "See how He came on the day of Pentecost! It is not carnal to pray that He may come again and that the place may be shaken. I believe that Pentecost was but a specimen day. I think the Church made this woeful mistake that Pentecost was a miracle never to be repeated. I have thought, too, that Pentecost was a miracle never to be repeated. I believe now, if we looked on Pentecost as a specimen day and began to pray, we should have the old Pentecostal fire here in Boston." Now some of us may find fault with Moody's viewpoint, but remember he lived in Pentecost!

It was to this fulness of the Spirit that our Lord invited us on the great feast day: *"If any man thirst, let him come unto me and drink. He that believeth on me, as the scripture hath said, from within him shall flow rivers of living water."* You will observe that our Lord sets forth here a simple process, a fivefold experience of thirsting, coming, drinking, believing and overflowing. If we are suffering from a defective experience of the Spirit it is because somewhere along that fivefold experience we have failed to appreciate or appropriate His Word.

Indeed, it is easy to see that most of us have failed at the very outset of this matter,—*" IF ANY MAN THIRST."* God has promised, *"I will pour out water upon him that is thirsty"* (Isaiah 44: 3), but who is thirsty? I talk with Christians who say they want more power and joy and peace and victory. But within a few minutes they have changed to some other subject, and soon some other topic is being discussed, and one feels that the fulness of the Spirit is, with them, just one of a variety of themes for polite after-dinner conversation. We poor Americans have become so shallow and superficial along all lines that we never really go deeply into any matter; we flit like butterflies from subject to subject, and never even in dreams have seen the things which are more excellent.

"IF ANY MAN THIRST ——" Just wanting a drink of water is not thirsting. We know nothing about thirst here in a land with water on tap at our elbows. Dr. Torrey tells us that he knew nothing of thirst until he was with soldiers of the Spanish-American war in camp, where dust filled the air day and night and where, as he put it, they ate

dust, drank dust, slept dust and dreamed dust, and there was no water anywhere fit to drink. Again, he was in China when cholera was raging and he could drink no water on the boat, but drank soft drinks as long as he dared, then lay all night suffering with thirst and thinking of his well at Northfield, far away. Ask some missionary to tell you what thirst is, when every pore of the body cries, "Water, water, water;" when the desert seems to be inside of you, and the lips swell, and every desire, hope and thought is just concentrated in one burning fever for a cooling drink. That is thirst, not just a casual, ordinary, normal inclination to drink water.

Do we know anything about that sort of spiritual thirst? Has your soul ever panted after the fulness of His Spirit as the hart pants after the water brooks? We are inclined nowadays to discount the agonies of the John Bunyans of another day who were so consumed with a vehement thirst for deeper blessing that food lost its taste and sleep could not be had. A more comfortable route to Beulah land has been discovered, but it is doubtful that men fully appreciate the blessedness of living in the eighth chapter of Romans who have not fully realized the bitterness of living in the seventh. It is true that some of these godly men of old unduly neglected the flesh, but we have unduly pampered the flesh, and it is clearly evident on all sides that a shallow thirst has brought a shallow satisfaction. It is quite true that God puts no special value on tears and all-night prayers and fastings, but He does reward a thirst so intense that time and food are forgotten and tears are not repressed. Very few Christians rejoice today with the deep joy of salvation, because they have never been deeply conscious of sin and, consequently, have no profound sense of deliverance. And it is just as true that few rejoice in fulness of the Spirit because, feeling self-sufficient, they have never known desperate thirst,—and one must thirst deeply to drink deeply. *"I will pour water upon HIM THAT IS THIRSTY."* Deep desire is followed by deep delight.

We live in a soft generation that lives on the surface and feeds at ethical soda fountains and spiritual delicatessen shops. If we are ever to know the profound, mountain-moving, soul-stirring torrents of living water surging upward into everlasting life, we must go deeper than pink-tea conversation and academic hair-splitting over theories of the baptism and filling of the Holy Ghost. We must join the company of men dreadfully, even though sometimes dismally, in earnest; who wrestled at Jabbok and came away with shrunken sinews but also as princes of God having power with God and men. The way to a personal and experimental Pentecost is not by a shallow and superficial prayer-meeting request for more power, easily uttered and soon forgotten; it is the road of a burning and blistering thirst that will not be denied; that importunes in spite of the mockery of feelings and the misunderstanding of friends and the misery of doubt and deadness and dulness until loaves have been granted from heaven and we have been set on fire to burn up for God. This road is not easy nor popular, and shorter cuts have been devised for those who will not pay the price; but, just as he who has forgiven most loved most, he who has thirsted most has been most deeply filled, and the fuller the fountain the mightier the rivers of living water that issue forth in torrents of blessing.

Pray, therefore, first of all, for a genuine thirst and a holy heartburn such as struck the Emmaus disciples of old; and look diligently into the mirror of the Word and wait patiently before the Lord that the Spirit may show you yourself in your awful need, your heart in its exceeding sinfulness, your life in its emptiness—that you may burn in raging fever and thirst for Him in His fulness.

Only then are you ready for the next move: "*If any man thirst, LET HIM COME UNTO ME.*" There must be a drawing near unto the Lord, not only in prayer, but in utter and absolute surrender. Everything that offends must be renounced, and we must lay all we are and have at His disposal. Not only must all be surrendered but abandoned—for surrender is not abandon, we do not always leave with Him what we commit to Him. We must be sure that we seek His blessing not for personal enjoyment, not just to boast about it, but for power in service. Just as wives often pray for the conversion of husbands not to the glory of God but only that they may have better husbands, so believers pray for fulness of the Spirit and have not because they ask amiss, that they may consume it on their lusts.

Now this matter of consecration, or surrender, or yielding, is one of those favourite topics of Christian conversation, part of that coinage of our speech which has grown familiar with much exchange, and yet, for all the handling, few of us examine it closely or know what image and superscription it bears. Christians march glibly to the front in our churches to "lay all on the altar" just as sinners file forward nowadays to "accept Christ," and then complain for the rest of their lives that they cannot see that it made any difference. It is no wonder! The depths have never been stirred, and so the depths have not been filled! We recognize that consecration as well as conversion outwardly may be manifested as quietly as an autumn sunset, but when one follows up the results of hundreds of public confessions and consecrations nowadays, he wishes there had been more noise. For all the sermons about the still, small voice, it is also well to remember that the Acts of the Apostles who turned the world upside down is not exactly what one would call a quiet book!

Coming to the Lord Jesus Christ in utter surrender and abandon for fulness of the Spirit is a profound experience that is second only to conversion, and it is amazing how men can profess it with far less concern than they go forward to receive a college diploma or marry a wife. Many who claim to follow Him are of the mixed multitude and soon turn back (Exodus 12: 38; Numbers 11: 4). Some are soon drawn away because of the uncounted cost, the unburied corpse and the unforsaken circle (Luke 9: 57–62). Our Lord does not commit Himself to such, for He knows what is in man (John 2: 23–25). Others "rededicate their lives," but the "high places" are not removed (I Kings 15: 14). Among others, the bushel of business and the bed of pleasure have not been taken from the candle of testimony (Mark 4: 21). In one way or another, superficial Christians come in shallow consecration, but they cannot drink deeply because, being still partly full of self, they cannot be completely filled with Him.

The whole matter goes back again to "*IF ANY MAN THIRST*." There is no way around that "*if*." Let a man thirst for water deeply enough and he will gladly renounce anything else for a drink. LET A MAN CRAVE THE FULNESS OF THE SPIRIT DEEPLY ENOUGH AND HE WILL GLADLY MAKE FULL SURRENDER. But this he must do, he must be emptied of all else to drink deeply of the Spirit.

And now the thirsting and the coming are followed by the drinking: "*If any man thirst, let him come unto me AND DRINK.*" Right here many earnest seekers grow sadly confused. We are so confirmed in the "seeing-is-believing" viewpoint that it is not easy for faith to receive what sight does not first perceive. Anyone who has experienced conversion, receiving Christ by faith for salvation, ought have no difficulty with this further step. Just as we receive the Saviour for forgiveness and sonship, just so do we receive the Holy Spirit for power in service. Of course, the Spirit came at Pentecost in a special sense at the beginning of the dispensation. Also, He regenerates the believer and indwells Him (John 3: 5, 6; I Corinthians 6: 19), and by the Spirit we are baptized into the body of Christ (I Corinthians 12: 13). The filling of the Spirit has been provided and should be ours from the very outset, but what is ours by provision is not always ours in conscious possession. Therefore, the Christian who, although saved, is conscious of lack of power and peace and joy must definitely appropriate the Spirit, receive the power, drink of the living water, just as he received Christ for salvation.

The Scriptures speak of being "*baptized*" with the Holy Spirit (Acts 1: 5), "*filled*" with the Spirit (Acts 2: 4; 4: 31), of the Holy Ghost "*falling*" upon believers (Acts 10: 44) and "*coming*" upon them (Acts 19: 6), and of believers "*receiving*" the Spirit (Acts 8: 17). Good men have differed greatly about the meaning of these terms. It has been pointed out that baptism is the act and the filling the result, just as a cup is filled when it is immersed. As usual, Christians have argued over the expressions more than they have enjoyed the experience. Just as we speak of regeneration as the work of God, and believing as the "under side"—our side of regeneration—so the experience of the Spirit's fulness is spoken of as a falling upon or coming upon believers from above, while the believer's part is, of course, the receiving. We cannot afford to minimize either side. There is much teaching today about "claiming promises" that would have us easily take what we want and go lightly along imagining we have it, only to realize down the road that we are acting a sort of glorified auto-suggestion and self-hypnosis. The emphasis is upon the subjective and not enough attention is paid God's side, the tremendous overwhelming from above. Many teachers discredit long prayers and waitings before the Lord, failing to see that, although sometimes they are false exercises, they are necessary to humble and quiet the believer before God and do indicate a real thirst. It is natural that this generation, not disposed to "wait" for anything, should prefer a quicker way to get the blessing with the least amount of trouble. But such short cuts tend to magnify the human side and obscure the stupendous truth that this blessing is God overwhelming men and submerging them in His flood tides of power, by which we become not mere pitchers to be filled but fountains sending forth torrents of living water. And the results of this teaching are evident today in rather tame experiences which, for all their receiving, seem poor products of Pentecost.

But it is also possible so to think of this blessing as a coming-down from above that men expect God to do it all, and so they wait and pray for what they should receive. When one genuinely thirsts, and has come to the Lord in utter surrender and abandon, and has waited until the depths have been sounded and the soul quieted, then we must drink, faith must appropriate the Spirit's filling.

"Drink" is not passive, it is something we are to do. The thirsting man might contemplate and appreciate water set before him, might wait before it for "something to happen," but the next thing to happen is for him to drink. Here earnest seekers have lost sleep and fasted and beaten their heads on the floor, even as Whitefield lived for some time on sage tea without sugar, and coarse bread, and prayed one night under a tree in the coldest weather, and practiced severe austerities in vain until he learned to look unto Christ. Others have fancied that they must have rare experiences like Finney, with waves of feeling like electricity sweeping hungry nerves, and so have dictated terms to the Lord. All this is beside the point. There must come that definite moment of contact when faith takes what the eye cannot see. It takes both giving and receiving to complete the gift. All God's giving without our receiving would be an incomplete transaction. To come to Christ and drink, therefore, is to receive, after the antecedent conditions have been met—the filling of the Spirit as provided and promised in the Word. It should be a fixed and definite step at a certain hour and moment, a clear-cut act of faith regardless of feeling.

Dr. Torrey waited for days in his study until the Lord spoke to his heart, "The blessing is yours. Now go and preach." Dr. Len G. Broughton tells of attending a convention after he entered the ministry and was convicted of powerlessness. Invited to come forward to kneel and surrender wholly to Christ and by faith accept the blessing, he went and received. A friend asked how he felt. "I didn't ask for feeling," he replied, "I was asking for the Holy Spirit." "How do you know you have anything more than you have had?" "I know it," he said, "just as I know I have Christ; I know it by faith." He had gone for filling, not feeling, and he received.

On this feast day our Lord not only invited us to drink, but said further: "*He that believeth on me, as the scripture hath said, from within him shall flow rivers of living water.*" "He that believeth on me" applies first of all, of course, to the initial faith in Christ for salvation, but it is also the secret of the Spirit-filled life. We are not only to drink of Christ in one initial filling of the Spirit but we are to drink and keep on drinking—"*being filled with the Spirit*"— and that is done by faith that continuously believes on Him and looks unto Him. Christ lives in the believer, and this life is lived "*by the faith of the Son of God*" (Galatians 2: 20).

Here is the supreme difficulty with earnest seekers after the fulness of the Spirit. Many have thirsted, have come to the Lord, have surrendered, have received the Spirit's filling, yet they dolefully lament that they see no difference; it did not last, the peace and power have departed. The reason is evident: they drank but they have not kept on drinking. "*He that believeth on me*" means more than believing on Him for the first filling; it means a continuous believing, an off-looking unto Jesus day by day. The rivers of living water are not flowing because the fountain of the heart is clogged and choked with doubt. "*YET BELIEVING, ye rejoice with joy unspeakable and full of glory*" (I Peter 1: 8). "*Said I not unto thee, that, if thou wouldest believe, thou shouldest see the glory of God?*" (John 11: 40).

Right at this point we fail to walk by faith and try to walk by sight. For a few days after receiving the blessing it is easy usually to walk in the light of the new experience. But soon one is struck with a dull mood; he may withdraw something that has been committed, or fail to obey on some point; he may look away from Jesus to his own feelings, circumstances, problems; he may have expected one filling to carry him through; he may become self-centered and seek merely to enjoy the blessing instead of overflowing in blessing to others. At any rate, crisis is not followed by continuance, and we forget that the same faith which appropriates the blessing at the outset keeps on drinking, so that the fountain keeps on springing up and overflowing in torrents of living water.

Our Lord said to the woman at Jacob's well: "*Whosoever drinketh of the water that I shall give him shall never thirst: but the water that I shall give him shall be in him a well of water springing up into everlasting life*" (John 4: 14). We are accustomed to speak of ourselves as empty vessels, to be filled each day with the Spirit, but that is not Scriptural. We are not empty pitchers to be refilled each morning: we are fountains that should evermore be springing up and overflowing, and our part is not to come empty each morning to be filled, but so to abide in Him by faith that we shall continually, night and day, be active channels of His Spirit. We are empty only as we allow the heart to be choked with sin, so that the stream cannot flow. It is not service that exhausts our power so that we need replenishing; sin clogs the inflow and needs to be removed. We are never emptied because of the outflow of blessing but because of trouble with the inflow of power.

So, as we drink and keep on drinking by believing on Him, there is the blessed experience of overflowing: "*From within him shall flow rivers of living water.*" This, our Lord said, is according to what the Scriptures had said. There is no such statement given verbatim in the Old

Testament, but the blessed figure of the well-watered life runs throughout. "*I will pour out my spirit upon you*" (Proverbs 1: 23). "*A fountain of gardens, a well of living waters*" (Song of Solomon 4: 15). "*I will open rivers in high places, and fountains in the midst of the valleys: I will make the wilderness a pool of water, and the dry land springs of water*" (Isaiah 41: 18). "*I will even make a way in the wilderness and rivers in the desert*" (Isaiah 43: 19). "*I will pour water upon him that is thirsty and floods upon the dry ground: I will pour my spirit upon thy seed, and my blessing upon thine offspring*" (Isaiah 44: 3). "*And the Lord shall guide thee continually, and satisfy thy soul in drought, and make fat thy bones: and thou shalt be like a watered garden, and like a spring of water, whose waters fail not*" (Isaiah 58: 11). "*I will pour out my spirit upon all flesh*" (Joel 2: 28).

Certainly the Scriptures describe for us a life continually well watered and abundant, a fountain springing up and overflowing. But when one looks around at most Christian lives, he sees not gardens with waters that fail not, but dried-up and unproductive hearts living in a spiritual drought, with only occasional showers of blessing, perhaps at the annual revival. In the Acts it was surprising to meet believers who were NOT filled with the Spirit (19: 1–7); now it is a surprise to meet a believer who IS filled with the Spirit!

And where is that exuberant joy of those who draw water from the wells of salvation? If these Jews at the feast could so rejoice over a hollow ceremony of pouring out water from Siloam that it was said "whoever has not witnessed it has never seen rejoicing at all," how hilarious should we be who drink of His living water! Leaving our figure of water for a moment, it is interesting to note that three times in the New Testament wine and the Holy Spirit are spoken of in the same connection. John the Baptist was not to drink wine but to be filled with the Spirit (Luke 1: 15); the Spirit-filled believers at Pentecost were accused of being full of new wine (Acts 2: 13); we are exhorted, "*Be not drunk with wine, wherein is excess; but be filled with the Spirit*" (Ephesians 5: 18). Wine changes the face, the walk, the talk, creates a commotion, and stimulates to hilarity, though it be a false joy; but the Holy Spirit fires the soul with heavenly wine and produces a holy hilarity. Immediately after reading in Ephesians, "*Be filled with the Spirit*" we read, "*Speaking to yourselves in psalms and hymns and spiritual songs, singing and making melody in your heart to the Lord*" (5: 19). There is the fountain overflowing with melodious joy!

It must ever be remembered that these rivers of living water must overflow in testimony and service. There is no reference to the blessing of the Spirit in the Bible that is not connected with its practical outflowing for the good of others. So long as this blessing is sought as an end in itself, it never can be obtained, because the purpose of it is to give power for service. It is not a true fountain that keeps its waters within itself and does not overflow. The primary purpose of His infilling is neither to make us holy nor happy, although it does both, but to empower us to testify and serve. If it does not issue in love for souls and testimony and faithful labour for the Lord, it is a false blessing. "Ye shall receive power, when the Holy Ghost is come upon you: and ye shall be my witnesses" (Acts 1: 8, R.V.).

Some think the gift of an evangelist is the mark of every Spirit-filled believer. Some think every one who has received must have a spectacular experience like Finney's, and fall into a trance or see visions. Others expect a certain rush of feeling or ecstasy of joy, and are disappointed when they must go on " dry faith," trusting the plain promise in the Word. But the manifestation of the Spirit is given to every man to profit withal, the Spirit dividing gifts to every man severally, as He will. We are not to dictate to Him the manner of His manifestation. It may take the form of a wonderful joy or a vision. It may issue in a quiet peace. We may see the evidence in new freedom in preaching or testimony, in greater results in soul-winning. There will be a manifestation, you may be sure of that. But ours is to drink and then believe the work is done because of the statement of the Word, leaving God to give the witness when and as He will.

The dissatisfaction so evident among Christians today arises, therefore, from many causes. Some have never really thirsted, so the satisfaction is shallow. Others have thirsted but have not come in utter surrender to the Lord or, if they have, they have not abandoned what has been committed, or else they have withdrawn something that was committed. Others have never taken the definite step of drinking, by faith receiving the filling. With some the fountain has become clogged by disobedience at some point, by failure to read the Word and pray, and by looking away from Christ to self. Others have sought the blessing for personal enjoyment, or have wanted some peculiar manifestation which the Spirit was not pleased to give. And perhaps by far the most have thought that one experience would automatically take care of everything from then on, instead of daily believing on Christ, yielding to Him, abiding in Him, keeping the channel clear so that Spirit may ever well up and out in rivers of living water. There is no experience which will, as if by magic, relieve us of the need of moment-by-moment looking unto Jesus, for then we would not need faith.

If the experience is defective, it is always because somewhere along this road of thirsting, coming, drinking, daily believing and overflowing, there has been neglect or disobedience. The doctrine is true: the defect lies somewhere in the lapse of duty.

Observe, finally, that the Spirit within the believer is "*a well of water springing up into everlasting life.*" Just as Christ in us is but the hope of glory, greater glory to come (Colossians 1: 27), and as the Spirit is the earnest of our inheritance, foretaste of more to follow (Ephesians 1: 14), so the Spirit-filled life ever increases from joy to joy, from power to more power, until it comes to perfection in heaven. "Spiritual life springs up toward its own perfection in eternal life." The Spirit-filled believer abounds more and more, day by day, in holiness and love and testimony and service, ever rising toward the glorious consummation in glory. "*The path of the just is as the shining light, that shineth more and more unto the perfect day*" (Proverbs 4: 18).

There is all the difference between this life of conscious power and peace and victory and the cheap "believism" current today,—as much difference as between the pouring out of the water from Siloam and the living waters of the Lord. This is no vague experience of trying to imagine that one has what it is more and more evident that he does not have. Whoever has known vividly this consuming thirst, who has come and received by true faith, not an easy assent to a fact, will find that the Spirit will soon bear witness with his spirit to the reality of the transaction. The confirmation will come: it may not come immediately; it may not come in blinding, dazzling fashion; it may not come in the manner expected or desired; but come it will if we drink and keep on drinking by simple faith in Him. Mind you, we are distinctly promised that we shall not thirst again (John 4: 14). If we have received and are still drinking, and the channels are clear, we shall never thirst again. That part of the experience need never be repeated. Meet His simple conditions, and you will be conscious day by day of His Spirit welling up into everlasting life and flowing out in rivers of living water. "Up" and "out," those are the two directions of His power, upward ever toward perfection, outward ever in streams of blessing.

Hear Him Who still stands among the hollow ceremonies of earth, the futile outpourings of water from Siloam, calling, "*Ho, every one that thirsteth, come ye to the waters.*" "*Let him that is athirst come. And whosoever will, let him take the water of life freely.*"

Printed in the United States of America